Joseph Grecian

History of the Eighty-third Regiment, Indiana Volunteer Infantry; for three years with Sherman

Joseph Grecian

History of the Eighty-third Regiment, Indiana Volunteer Infantry; for three years with Sherman

ISBN/EAN: 9783337305154

Printed in Europe, USA, Canada, Australia, Japan

Cover: Foto ©ninafisch / pixelio.de

More available books at **www.hansebooks.com**

HISTORY

OF THE

EIGHTY-THIRD REGIMENT,

INDIANA VOLUNTEER INFANTRY.

FOR THREE YEARS WITH SHERMAN.

COMPILED FROM

THE REGIMENTAL AND COMPANY BOOKS, AND
OTHER SOURCES, AS WELL AS FROM THE
WRITER'S OWN OBSERVATIONS
AND EXPERIENCE.

WRITTEN IN THE "FIELD" AND IN THE "SHELTER-TENT."

NEAR WASHINGTON, D. C., JUNE 3, 1865.

By J. GRECIAN,

OF COMPANY A

CINCINNATI
JOHN F. UHLHORN, PRINTER
74 WEST THIRD STREET.
1865.

PREFACE.

In offering a history of the 83d Regiment Indiana Volunteer Infantry to the public, I do not feel that I am called upon for an apology. That I should "get up" such a history, was suggested to me by a Sergeant of Company G, while on picket with him, and all, both officers and men, said "write it." So, of course, I could not reasonably either refuse or neglect to make the best effort in my power, under the circumstances in which I was placed. It has been accomplished in the shelter-tent, or in the open air, surrounded by my noisy comrades, and it has cost me some pains-taking to procure correct data, and to arrange it; and I feel assured that my difficulties in this respect will be appreciated. If any mistake should appear, I hope it will be attributed to these difficulties I have labored under in "the work." Some things may not appear so plain as might be desired, but I have endeavored to make as plain and as full a history as possibly could be got into so small a compass.

It has been urged by a few that deserters should be exposed to the public, but the majority are of a different opinion. Indeed, there are but very few of those who deserted from our Regiment that did not repentantly return, and were restored to duty and favor.

I would tender my hearty thanks to those officers and men who have afforded me so much encouragement and even assistance in this, my first and only work of the kind.

If the friends of the 83d Indiana shall, in this little work, find a satisfactory record of our campaining and of our suffering, as a Regiment, in the cause of our Country, I shall be amply rewarded in my efforts for their information.

Respectfully, your Obed't Serv't,

J. GRECIAN,
Co. A, 83d Ind. Vols., Inft.

CHAPTER I.

This efficient and well renowned Regiment came out under the call of the President for 600,000 troops, in 1862. Its place of rendezvous was Lawrenceburg, Indiana, in the Fourth District of our noble State, whose soldiers are behind in no respect, either in the manual of arms, or on the fatigueing march, or in the bloody conflict on the battle field, against our malignant foes. It was organized in the month of August, 1862, by Col. Benj. Spooner, whose superior talents as a military officer is well known in the army, as well as to the people at home in the State, and who was loved and cheerfully obeyed by every man in the Regiment, while he continued its commander, which was, until he lost his left arm in that bloody charge on the rebel works at Kenesaw Mountain, on the 27th day of June, 1864.

Some of the companies of our Regiment were enlisted with the expectation and intention of going into the 68th Indiana Volunteers; and indeed one company (B) was in that Regiment at "Camp Logan," near Greensburg, Indiana. But, having the privilege given them by the commander of the camp, they voted themselves out of the 68th, and went into "Camp Ross," with part of Company I, which had been in Camp Logan about a week; and Company A, which went into camp on the 12th of

August, arriving in Camp Logan about 2 o'clock P. M., too late to get into the 68th, and so were ordered to "Camp Ross" the same evening.

The next day Company A held its election for officers. The captaincy was balloted for by Samuel P. Chipman and Orin T. Darling, which two, had an equal claim to the office, as having been equally successful in enlisting the men composing the company; indeed, they both, for some time, had command of a squad of "Home Guards," one at Milan, the other at Delaware, Ripley county. Chipman was elected on the first ballot, it being the understanding that the one not getting the majority for Captain, was to be considered elected First Lieutenant. To this all were agreed. Wm. H. Snodgrass was elected Second Lieutenant by acclamation. This election was superintended by J. Skeene, U. S. A. Marshal.

When it was found that Company A could not get into the 68th, Governor Morton was consulted by telegraph, and he, upon being assured that another Regiment could be raised in ten days, authorized the organization of the "83d Regiment."

Company A, when it went into camp, numbered 101 men, all told; Company B, 101 men; Company C, 94 men; Company E, 97 men; Company F, 94 men; Company G, 102 men; Company H, 100 men; Company I, 96 men; Company K, 89 men, all told; this includes officers and men. Company D was still wanting to make the Regiment complete, which was still the case when the Regiment left camp for the field, on the 7th day of November. Company D was finally supplied at Memphis, Tennessee, after we had made our "Tallahatchie" march, and returned to that place. It was made up of men drafted for nine months, and so left us again at the expiration of their time, the next September. We have no direct means of giving the history of Company D, because there is none of its books with the Regiment at this time, and, in fact, the strict propriety of placing its history with that of a Volunteer Regiment might be questioned, although we do not feel that our Regiment was at all disgraced by the connection and services of that Company, for it was composed of noble, brave men. They did good and valiant service for their country while " in the service."

On the 18th day of August, Companies A and B, with that part of Company I that was with them in " Camp Ross," moved " by rail " to Camp Laz. Noble, the place of rendezvous for the Regiment, situated on the Whitewater Canal, just at the east side of Lawrenceburg, Indiana. They found Company G already in camp, and, by the 25th, all the companies were in, except Company K, which did not get its full number till late in September, too late to be mustered into the U. S. Service at the same time the other companies were. This was done by Captain W. Cheek, U. S. Mustering Officer for the Fourth District, on the 25th of September.

Thus, we see the beginning of this powerful Regiment, which has commanded the respect of our country, and has elicited the praise of many officers and war-worn veterans, and even General Sherman, when he received our Regiment at Memphis, Tennessee, on the 11th day of November, 1862, said, "I never saw a better looking regiment of men in all my life." In Camp Laz. Noble "the boys" took their first lesson in the "drill," and enjoyed for the first time, (most of them,) the "soft things" of a soldier's life.

Though the time we spent here in our "camp of instruction" was rendered pleasant by the oft repeated visits of friends, ladies, and patriots, who came laden with the rich fruits of husbandry, served up in the best style of our western housewives, yet we felt that we had left our homes to engage in hard campaigning for three long years, many of us never to return or behold the smiles of loved ones around the family board, or enjoy the pleasures of a social circle of home friends. This is what many a noble youth has realized, while those at home are left to weep the loss of patriot friends, now slumbering in southern shades, or near the brink of some stream that continues to murmur their requiem of praise and honor, from Memphis, Tennessee, and Arkansas Post, to the Atlantic coast, where McAllister once "frowned down on the flag of the free." Those were times of "social joy and parting farewells," that all of us have often thought of with renewed courage as we have been facing dangers unknown to all, except soldiers, and as we have marched, hungry and weary, through heat and dust, or through darkness and mud, through storms and through swamps; and as with sleepless vigilance we have watched for the encroachments of the foe, or, without shelter, have layed in the wild woods, or sat by our bivouac during a rainy night, or have lain in the ditch, or worked all night to secure ourselves from the hissing shells, and the flying missiles of death.

When the Regiment was organized and filled up, the "Field and Staff" officers were: Colonel, Benjamin J. Spooner; Lieut.-Colonel, Jas. H. Cravens; Major, James S. Jelley; Lieutenant George B. Robinson, Regimental Adjutant; First Surgeon, Samuel Davis; First Assistant Surgeon, Wm. Gillispie; Second Assistant Surgeon, Henry C. Vincent; First Lieutenant George D. Late, Q. M. Others, at different times, served our Regiment as Surgeons with acceptance and success. Among these we love to mention the names of Dr. Cornelius B. Carr, of the 29th Illinois Volunteers, and Dr. Samuel Weaver, of Dillsborough, Indiana, and others; but the journal and general summary of the Regiment will show who those men were that filled that important place in our Regiment at different times. The tables of companies will show who the line officers were at first, and who were at different times promoted.

The officers of all the companies being elected, they proceeded at once, and daily, to drill their men, most of whom were very quick to learn the "tactics" of Hardee's code. Some drill, either company, squad, or battalion, was performed four times each day, unless stormy weather prevented it; for Colonel Spooner was careful of the health of his men, which is one of the most necessary things in the commander of any troops, if their comfort or efficiency is taken into account. This was kept up until the Regiment left for the "theater of war," which it did on the 7th day of November, 1862.

There are several things connected with our stay in the camp of instruction worthy of note. First: In the latter part of August there was quite a stir through the country on account of a rumor that the rebels were making a raid through Kentucky, and were approaching the Ohio River somewhere in our vicinity, or near Cincinnati, Ohio. This gave a fine opportunity for our regimental officers to play off a nice joke. So on the evening of the 25th, all the men had gone to bed, and the most of them were already asleep, when suddenly we were aroused by the startling order, "Fall in! fall in! hurry up! fall in!" This done, companies A and G were ordered "forward." By some means Captain Morris with his company had got ahead of Capt. Chipman. They called out, one to the other, "where are we ordered to go?" "I don't know," was the reply. "Forward!" shouted both captains to their men, all of whom declared their readiness to go anywhere with their officers. They proceeded out of camp toward town, when by the canal, the Adjutant came galloping up behind us and shouted "halt, where are you going? I did not order you here." A pause ensued, and he ordered "forward." We proceeded to the Depot, and having drawn some old guns, we retired to camp, went to bed, and slept till morning, then got up to reflect on the excitement of the previous night, and thus go on in the regular routine of duty. This was done, probably at the instigation of Colonel Spooner and the Adjutant, to see what effect it would have on the men, whether they would flinch at a little danger or not, but they found all ready for duty in apparent danger, as other times they have been ready for duty in times of real danger.

Another thing that deserves note, is the zeal and faithfulness with which "the boys" did picket duty along the Ohio River, and at the Rail Road Bridge across the Miami River, as different companies were sent out on duty in those times of supposed danger. And several companies were sent down the River, and stationed at different points in the vicinity of Rising Sun, Indiana, to steady the nerves of the people in those parts, who were uneasy on account of the real or supposed danger they were in from the above mentioned raiders. These companies were, C, B, E and G, but nothing of note occurred, only "the boys" were well entertained by the citizens, and came back to camp in fine spirits, after an absence of about ten days.

About the 5th of October the Regiment was armed with Belgian rifles, with sabre bayonets; these guns were awkward and heavy, carrying two ounce cartridges. We carried and used these guns for about one year. On the 11th day of October the whole Regiment was furloughed home, to attend the State elections, only leaving six men of each company to take care of camp. All returned to camp on the 16th. This was the last furlough given at Camp Laz. Noble, except to those who had taken care of the camp during our absence, and to a very few others on special occasions.

Having been paid $25 bounty, and the monthly wages up to the first of November, the Regiment started on the 7th for "Dixie's Land," to engage in hard campaigning and bloody conflict on the battle field. We arrived at Cairo by rail, at 2 A. M. of the 9th, having passed Indianapolis, Greencastle, and Terre Haute in the night of the 7th, and through Southern Illinois during the 8th. The Regiment reported at Fort Pillow, on board the steamer Dacotah, at about 2 P. M. of the 9th, and arrived at Memphis on the 10th, at 5 P. M., but did not get off the boat until the next morning at 7. We reached Camp "Ben. Spooner" at about 12 M., feeling the weight and inconvenience of the "knapsack" for the first time. We were received by Major-General Sherman the same day.

Our camp was situated close by the city of Memphis, and on the east side. Here we spent our time pleasantly until the 26th of the month, while the troops were collecting in, who were to form an army to be thrown against the rebels at Vicksburg, and in Mississippi "in general." We received orders on the evening of November 25th, to be ready to march the next morning at 8 o'clock, but did not march till 30 minutes after; but we were drawn up "in line" and some orders were read to us, in which we were informed that we were placed in the 3d Brigade, 2d Division, 15th Army Corps, in which relation we have stood during our whole stay in the army, except that we were changed from the 3d to the 2d Brigade, in about two weeks after the organization of the 15th Army Corps.

CHAPTER II.

At 8 o'clock on the morning of November 26th we were in line according to orders, and at 30 minutes after 11 A. M., we set out on our first march, the one commonly known as that of the Tallahatchie. We should have stated that our sick were left in Overton Hospital, and other places in the city of Memphis. We marched sixteen miles that day, and at sunset went into camp at Germantown, Tennessee. At 7 A. M. on the 27th we resumed our march, halting ten minutes for rest in each hour; this was done by the order of Brig. Gen. M. L. Smith, who was in command of our Division. This was continued till one o'clock, when we halted till 4 P. M., then resumed the march till 8, when we went into camp in a cornfield, having made about 18 miles during the day. Next morning we moved at 9.30, and at night we camped at Coldwater Creek, after having marched about 15 miles. We made slow progress on the 28th till 5 P. M., and then pushed rapidly forward until 11, then halted in a newly plowed field. A heavy rain fell during the latter part of the night, and made our camp muddy enough by morning. On the 29th we moved 9 miles. At 9 A. M. of the 30th we moved on, and halted at 6 P. M. at Tullahoma, Mississippi; here we camped again in a cornfield. About the time we had got our tents up, there came one of those storms of wind, thunder and rain, for which the South is so much noted. The wind blew for an hour, and left scarcely a tent standing, and the rain came down in torrents, and we were nearly all inundated. The next day, December 1st, we did not move, but were not allowed to rest, for our brigade commander, Colonel David Stewart, took occasion to drill his command during the afternoon, and at dark we returned to camp, and at 1 o'clock A. M. of the 2d of December, we marched toward the Tallahatchie River, 12 miles distant, reaching it about noon, the day being stormy, and the rain turning to snow before night. We halted at Wiatt and went into camp, and set about building a bridge across the river, for the rebels had destroyed the ferry at that point, and all the bridges up and down the Tallahatchie as far up as Abbeville, near which the rebels, under General Price, had been for some time intrenched, and from which position Genereal U. S. Grant had, a day or two previous to our arrival, driven them and taken possession of it.

On the morning of December 15th we crossed the river on our newly made bridge, and moved about 6 miles, to the vicinity of Bowles' Mills, which were taken possession of, and used to grind meal for the army during their stay at this point. We remained at this point, for the rebels had fled before General Grant's forces, going south, and being pursued by General Grant's forces, those of General Sherman stopping as above stated. We should state that Major James S. Jelly had remained for a day or two at Memphis after our marching, in order to attend to some business pertaining to the regiment, in endeavoring to return was overtaken by guerrillas, and robbed of his horse, saddle, holsters, sword and all other arms and valuables. They then took him back to Germantown, and having paroled him, permitted him to follow the regiment.

On the 10th of December we started on our return march to Memphis; we reached the town of Wiatt that evening and the next day moved on toward Memphis, by a somewhat shorter route than that by which we had formerly marched, and reached that city about noon of the 13th, and went into camp at the north side of the city, (having marched 150 miles,) where we remained till the 20th, which was a terribly rainy time, and our camp became almost insufferably muddy. We were also joined by Lieutenant Colonel James H. Cravens, who brought with him Company D, with their officers in charge, and their knapsacks well stored, and all ready for a hard winter's campaign.

On the morning of the 20th of December, we again decamped, and moved to the wharf, where a fleet of about 60 steamers and several gunboats were waiting to conduct the army down the Mississippi River to the hostile city of Vicksburg. At this time our Regiment was again deprived of the services of a considerable number of men, for measles had got into the ranks, and many had been taken, and some died of this dangerous disease, among whom was James, the only son of Stephen S. Merrill. He was a noble youth, possessing too much refinement and genius for a common soldier. His loss is felt not only by his parents, (or rather by his mother, now widowed,) but also by the whole community where he lived. He belonged to Company A. We got on board of the old steamer Sioux City, which was as "leaky as all out of doors," and which was our only house, and the only shelter we had for near four stormy, inclement weeks. So, on the evening of the 20th of December, we again found ourselves moving down the broad bosom of the "Father of Waters." Nothing of interest occurred as the fleet moved slowly down the deep-rolling current, stopping frequently to take on rails or wood, the former being scarce, and often the soldiers had to cut the latter from the green stumps. The boats did not run at all of nights, on account of the danger of being attacked by guerrillas. Thus, on the afternoon of the 26th, we landed at Johnson's plantation, at the mouth of the Yazoo River, 12 miles from the Mississippi. Old River, properly, connects the two rivers, Yazoo and Mississippi. There we disembarked at 4 P. M., and moved out two miles, and stopped for the night in a swamp, much grown up with thorns and green briars; this was also a rainy night, and we got but little rest or sleep; and the next morning we began moving at about 9 o'clock. Skirmishing being renewed—for it had been going on in front the evening before—by noon it had reached the warmth of battle indeed. At 4 P. M. we reached our position on the right of our army, in front of the enemy, who occupied a strong fortified position on the heights, at the east side of the large valley through which runs Chickasaw Bayou, across which the battle was fought, principally on the 28th of December, 1862, that proved so disastrous to our forces. At the moment we were coming into our position from the rear of Gen. Steele's Division, we were hotly engaged, and succeeded in taking a battery from the enemy, but were compelled to retire again with heavy loss, giving up the guns they had so valiantly taken. We remained on the line all night, being in the standing timber, with an abattis in our front, between us and the rebel line. The enemy poured several volleys of musketry into us during the night, and awhile before daylight next morning began throwing shells at us. Thus we were aroused to a lively sense of our "situation," and for the first time were called on to "lay down." At 9 A. M., we advanced in line of battle, and took position in the above mentioned abattis, the enemy pouring their fire into our ranks as we advanced, and we returned it as hotly as they sent it to us. We soon made them hide behind their works. We continued in the engagement till about 4 P. M., when we were relieved by the 6th and 8th Missouri Regiments. In this engagement our Regiment lost one officer and three men killed, (the officer was Lieutenant Bridges, of Company E,) and 15 wounded, one of whom was Adjutant Robinson, severely, in the shoulder. The battle was continued the next day, but we were not engaged, and lay in reserve; at night a heavy rain fell, continuing all night, and we suffered greatly from wet and cold, for we could not kindle fires on account of drawing the enemy's fire. All night of the 31st our Regiment was engaged in building redoubts, and mounting two batteries, one of 20-pounder Parrott guns, the other of brass howitzers. But the next day, (the 1st of January, 1863,) was passed without fighting, and that night our forces evacuated their position, and returned to the boats on the Yazoo, about six miles distant. On the 2d of January, the fleet moved to Milligan's Bend, and lay there till the morning of the 6th, and then moved up the river, arriving at the mouth of White River on the 7th. Thence, on the 9th, we moved up White River 10 or 12 miles, thence through a bayou, or cut-off, into the Arkansas River, thence up that narrow, crooked stream to within four miles of the "Old Arkansas Post." Here the rebels occupied a strong fort and two or three lines of works. We disembarked on the afternoon of the 10th, and before dark we were again under rebel fire. We lay all night under the mouths of their guns, and they continued for several hours to throw shells into our ranks, killing some in ours, and other regiments. By day light of the 11th, all the troops were in line, forming a complete connection around the enemy. The rebels were engaged during the night in preparing for the assault, which took place about 1 P. M., and lasted till 4 P. M., when the enemy surrendered. This was a sharp fight. Four of our gunboats were in the engagement, and soon succeeded in smashing up and silencing all the guns of the fort.

Our land batteries were equally successfull, and 7,100 prisoners and 8,000 stand of arms, with all their artillery, stores, ammunition, etc., fell into our hands. Thus we felt greatly encouraged with our victory, though we had not succeeded in our first fight, (that of Chickasaw Bayou.) The Arkansas Post affair was a severe one, the night was very frosty, and no one was allowed to kindle a fire, and many never recovered from the effects of cold they endured that night. In this fight our Regiment lost 4 men killed and 19 wounded. In this battle, as also it had in that of Chickasaw Bayou, "the 83d" gained great credit. Colonel Spooner only said to his men, "Remember your State, forward!" and they always remembered and congratulated themselves on the thought that they were from Indiana.

On the 15th of January we were on board of the steamer and descending the Arkansas River, and arrived at Napoleon, where we stayed till the 18th. On the night of the 15th there fell a heavy snow storm, which lay on the ground all day of the 16th, to the depth of 8 or 10 inches. This rendered our old boat any thing but comfortable. One-half, at least, of the Regiment was attacked with sickness, from which many never recovered. Some were sent up the Mississippi River to hospitals at the North. Others remained with the Regiment only to drag out a few short weeks in misery, and then be buried on the levee at Young's Point. We arrived at Young's Point, or rather opposite the mouth of the Yazoo, or Old River, on the 21st of January, and the next day disembarked, and went into camp near Butler's Canal, commenced by that General about a year previous to our occupation of the spot. Upon this canal we were engaged, digging it out deep and wide, and throwing up a levee on each side, so that when finished, it would admit boats to pass through, and thus get below the batteries and forts on the "hills of Vicksburg." but the water continued to rise so the canal proved a failure, and by the 8th of March it became necessary for us to move our camp off the bottom, or rather "swamp," and crowd our tents on the levee, so as to prevent being inundated.

Our stay here in this dismal, swampy valley, from the 22d of January till the above named date, and, in fact, till the 1st of May following, was one of unparalleled discouragement. Scarcely a man had any thing like good health; about one-half were prostrated with various diseases, many dying almost daily. Others were sent to hospitals at the North, some of whom died there, and others did not return to the Regiment for a year or even more; also many were discharged on account of disability, and so were lost to the Regiment. In fact, these were the worst times the 15th Army Corps ever saw, for the sickness was general, and the soldiers continued to die off by hundreds, and the levee for miles is almost one continued mass of graves. We were compelled to pitch our tents on newly made graves while we remained on the levee, and in some cases the stench of the decomposing bodies was quite perceptible. Under these circumstances it is not strange that many good soldiers should become discouraged, and feel hard toward the General Government, that at all other times, both before and after, always stood up in the dignity of true patriotism, and fought, suffered, and sustained all the measures of the Executive, to crush out the rebellion, without any exception. And here a word of honor is due to Col. Spooner. He saw and felt the peril of those times of special distress, and took timely measures to encourage his men and save their untarnished reputation. On the fourth day of February, he made an oration, and took a vote in the Regiment, and no man voted to do any other way than to prosecute the war vigorously until the rebellion should be entirely put down, and the authority of the Constitution and General Government should be "established in all the States;" and every patriot is willing to acknowledge the wisdom of the step he then took.

Some other notes of these times are not out of place in this connection. On the morning of Feb. 1st, the Queen of the West ran the blockade of the rebel batteries at Vicksburg; then for the first time we were awakened from our slumbers, by the thunder of their huge guns, which belted at her with all fury, but did her little injury, for she ran so fast down the current, and worked her guns on them with such effect, that they did not succeed in getting good range on her until she was past and out of their reach. This brought a halo of cheers from "the boys" as they saw her come round the bend of the river below; for in this they saw the beginning of that success which was afterwards to be theirs in their operation against the enemy at that time occupying those hills that frowned down on them with so much defiance from the opposite side of the great Mississippi.

At another time all were aroused by the bellowing of those guns against a supposed "Turretted Monster" passing down the river. Gen. Grant had adopted a plan to find the position of all the enemy's batteries, and an old hull of a boat was accordingly fixed up with some barrels placed one on another, with sawdust on fire at the bottom, the smoke ascending out at the top to represent smokstacks. Turrets of lumber were also constructed and all was painted black so as to make the appearance of a formidable "Turretted Monster," as it thus floated down the current in the darkness of the night. As it came in range of their guns, they all opened on it with their utmost vengence, and General Pemberton also sent a dispatch to the crew of the Indianola, another iron-clad ram of the first class that had only a week or so previously fallen into their hands by some unfortunate circumstance, to blow her up so as to prevent her from being retaken by this formidable "monster."

On the evening of April 17th, a fleet of five or six iron-clads and six or eight transports, with wet bales of hay hung all round so as to resist the force of cannon shots, and prevent shell from entering their hulls and cabins, started down past those formidable batteries, which consisted of about sixty guns of large calibre. As soon as this fleet came in range they were attacked by the rebel batteries. The gunboats immediately returned the fire, and now the "cannons deep roar" became terrific. No man could count the number of shots fired, either by the rebel batteries, or by the iron-clads, which succeeded in so confusing the enemy that they only destroyed one of our transports. All the rest of the fleet got by with but little damage.

Blockade running had now become a familiar thing, and the "Yanks" were getting a sufficient force of both iron-clads and troops below the "batteries" to destroy the rebel fleet up Red river, and establish a post at the mouth of it, which compelled the rebels to destroyed part of their fleet on that stream and all they had on Black river.

Another thing worthy of note during our stay on Young's Point, is the eagerness with which the "convalescents" (and all were such except those too ill to get around,) gathered and devoured the various kinds of greens and other eatables that grew so abundantly there, even at that early season. Fish and even lobsters were sought and gathered in quantities. These things greatly aided in restoring health and strength to many in the absence of other sanitaries, which soon after began to arrive in quantities.

CHAPTER III.

On the morning of March 17th, our division left camp on the levee at Young's Point, and getting aboard of transports, we ascended the Mississippi to Eagle's Bend, thence we marched across a neck of land, and thence ascended the various bayous till we reached Deer Creek, thence disembarking we marched fifteen miles, and within three miles of the Rolling Fork of Big Sunflower river. At this point five of our gunboats were blockaded and beleagued by the rebels as they were trying to get through Black Bayou into the Sunflower, and so into the Yazoo river above the rebel batteries at Hains' Bluffs. This was called "The Black Bayou March or Trip."

Having driven the enemy and rescued the ironclads, on Sunday the 23d, we returned toward the landing on Monday, and a heavy rain fell during the whole of Sunday night, and continued falling all day Monday until 2 P. M., about which time we halted to wait for the gunboats, for the rebels had felled so much timber into the Bayou that it was difficult for them to get along. This day we had to plod through rain and mud, at times almost up to our knees. The ground through which we marched was swampy and interspersed with huge canebrakes. This was sufficient to try the strength of the best constitution. But this was not all, for after we had reached the landing about 2 P. M. of Tuesday, the 25th, our regiment was ordered to go back about three miles to meet the rebels, who had been following us, and engage them and ascertain their strength, and if possible, "draw them on" a little way, so that the gunboats could get range on them; but this we failed to do. We, or rather companies A and F waded a swamp for near a mile, the water being very cold, and about three feet deep. Soon after we got out of this, we found a force of the enemy halted in a large field, and a skirmish of half an hour ensued, in which we lost one man in company G, he was shot dead on the spot. We soon fell back, but the rebels did not follow us; so after dark we returned to the landing.

On Wednesday we got on board of the transports, which reached "Steel's Bayou" that night, and the next day, the 27th, we arrived at our camp on the levee at Gains' Point, after an absence of ten days.

We found Dr. Vincent, assistant surgeon, very ill with typhoid fever, from which he did not recover so as to resume his duties in the regiment during the whole summer, and in the fall of 1863, he resigned on account of his inability to endure the hardships and exposures of the field, and his place was taken, and also Dr. Gillespie's place, who had been chosen to take charge of the small pox hospital, situated on Paw-Paw Island, by Dr. J. C. Anthony, of the 127th Ill. Vols. This man continued with our Regiment until some time in the latter part of the summer, and then Dr. —— Keller of the 6th Missouri Vols., was assigned to us, and after this a doctor from some other regiment was with us until Dr. Gillespie returned to us in October, Dr. Sam Davis, having then resigned.

We moved camp about the 1st of April off the levee and went into regular camp further up the Valley. Here we had ground a little higher than that we had previously occupied. There the health of the soldiers somewhat improved. On the 13th of April we received four months pay— up to February 28th, 1863.

We remained quietly in this camp, the Regiment going some three or four days to work on a canal then being made about six miles above. This was another scheme probably to divert the attention of the rebel General at Vicksburg, but ostensibly for the purpose of getting a safe passage for transports through to the Mississppi river below.

On the 29th of April, our division again went on board of the transports, and ascended the Yazoo to Hains' Bluffs, and made a demonstration, or show of attack on the rebels, who were strongly fortified at this place as well as at all other points that were considered accessible in gaining a foothold against Vicksburg. There occured a considerable fight between their batteries and our gunboats, on the 30th. The Chocktaw, especially did them damage, dismounting several of their largest guns. We withdrew that night, and on the 1st of May we returned to Gains' Point. This was done to draw the force of the enemy up there, and so favor Gen. Grant's operations at Grand Gulf. We arrived in camp at dark, and the next morning we decamped, moving by transports to Milligen's Bend, La., and on the next day we went into camp at that place, and remained there until the 7th, when we set out to join Gen. Sherman, east of Black River, by way of Richmond, La., and by Grand Gulf. We crossed the Mississippi at that place on the evening of the 11th, having passed through a beautiful part of the country on our way thither. The Regiment resumed its march next morning, and continued it each day, marching from fifteen to twenty miles per day, through a most beautiful country, lying east of Black river, until we arrived at Raimond on the 15th of May, at 5 P. M. On the 16th, the battle of Champion Hills was fought, but our Regiment was not engaged, but was in line in reserve nearly all day, and after night we continued moving about until about 9 o'clock, and then went into camp on the battle-field. On the morning of May 18th, we crossed Black river, and at 2 P. M. began skirmishing with the enemy near their outer line of works in the rear of Vicksburg. The forenoon of the 19th was taken up in skirmishing with the rebels, and at 2 P. M. a general charge was made on their works. It was a bloody affair, and resulted in a heavy loss. The 83d lost two captains killed, (Calvert of company C, and Chrisvell of company K) and one captain, (Chipman of company A) wounded, and twenty-two men killed and wounded. Among the killed was James H. Cleveland, of company A. He was a minister of the Universalist faith. He was a very worthy man and an eloquent orator, and in him his friends lost a most kind hearted man, and the country a philosopher of no ordinary grade. On the 20th our Regiment was sent to guard the supply train, and build a corduroy road and bridge the Chickesaw Bayou, so as to get supplies from the fleet on the Yazoo river. On the 21st the Regiment returned to the front, arriving about midnight, hungry and weary, having not slept or rested of any account for several days and nights. On the 22d of May another general charge was made on the rebel works, but with the same result as on the 19th, and our loss was heavier.

The company tables will show the names of all that fell in this as well as in all other fights the Regiment has ever been in. There was a large party of men detailed and that volunteered from our Division on the 22d, to storm a fort immediately in their front. In our regiment they all volunteered. They were Corporal Daniel Langwell, of company A; David Helms, of company B; John Conway, of company C; —— Armstrong, of company D; Joseph France, of company E; Reuben Smally, of company F; Frank Stolly and William Stienmetz, of company G; Thomas Blazedwell, of company H; William Chisman, of company I, and Jacob Overturf, of company K, were the men in the 83d that volunteered to storm the fort. Each man took with him a pole, rail or plank, of which to construct some means by which to cross the deep ditch in front, and to scale the fort. Some of them succeeded in getting into the fort, but were compelled to fall back, for they could not stay (alive) any length of time on it. In this charge there was a cannon ball passed through our colors taking out some of "the stars."

General Sherman in his official report bears witness to the valor of the 83d Indiana, and states that her flag was formost and went further than any other in our division.

Affairs now settled down into a regular seige, which lasted until the 4th of July, when the rebels being almost literally "starved and dug out," surrendered.

On the morning of May 26th, our regiment with several others started to scour the country from Hains' Bluffs, (then in our possession) to Yazoo City, in search of the enemy under General Joe Johnson, said to be in those parts. They reached Mechanicsburg through a fine country, and on the 31st returned to Hains' Bluffs, at which place we rested two days, and then returned to "the front." Up to the 4th of July artillery firing and sharp-shooting was kept up continually, except for two and half hours on the 24th of May, when a flag of truce was allow, in order to bury the dead The troops were worked hard all this time. All regiments furnished details to work in the sapps and mines, both day and night. On the 20th of June, 360 pieces of artillery were worked as fast as could be done with safety, for six hours against the rebels. The gunboats and mortars in the river were also engaged at the same time; and in fact there had been eight mortars kept at work during all the seige, and thousands of shells had been thrown into the city, compelling the citizens to keep closely in their bomb-proofs. Thus on the 4th of July, 1863, ended this dreadful seige, the rebels being able to hold out no longer, and for a long time, had only "mule meat" for their daily rations.

On the morning of July 6th our regiment, with most of the army, started to meet Johnson's forces coming to relieve General Pemberton's army at Vicksburg. We fell in with the rebel pickets on the east side of Black river. The enemy fell back and were pursued by our forces to Jackson, the capital of the State of Mississippi. Here there occurred a considerable fight, but the rebels fell back across Pearl river, and our forces after destroying all that could be of use to the enemy, retired to the west side of Black river, and organized "Camp Sherman." This was done on the 26th day of August, 1863, the troops having arrived there on the 25th. This camp was situated in a nice shady road, about 14 miles east of Vicksburg, Mississippi, and in this pleasant camp we staid till the 20th day of September. During this "recess" of hostilities, five per cent. of the Regiment was fuloughed home, among whom were the men that volunteered in the storming party at Vickburg, on the 22d day of May. Colonel Spooner also visited his home on leave of absence, as he had done once before, while we were at Young's Point. Lieutenant-Colonel Myers, also obtained a leave of absence for 20 days, and visited his home, leaving Major Jacob Eggleston in command of the regiment. We were not permitted to lay still in idleness, however, but were exercised on drill or review each day. This was necessary for the health of the men.

On the 20th of September, our Regiment was sent out seven miles from camp, to picket a crossing of Black river, and on the 23d returned to the division, and then moved to the railroad crossing six miles below, on the same river.

CHAPTER IV.

On the 27th of September, we started on another campaign. We arrived at Vicksburg, 15 miles, and got on board of the steamer "City of Pekin" the same afternoon, and that night began to ascend the Mississippi River ; the 29th and 30th were mostly spent in wooding the fleet ; and now, for the first, we heard of the heavy battle of Chickamauga ; on the 3d of October, we landed, for a short time, at Helena, Arkansas. The water was very low, and the fleet had some difficulty in getting over the shoals, just above Helena, but on the 4th we disembarked at Memphis, Tennessee, where we remained in camp, east of the city, till the 8th. On the 7th, we turned over our old guns and drew new "Springfield" rifles ; we started on our "long march" on the morning of the 8th, but we were destined to be detained in our progress by bands of Rebel cavalry. We took the train at Memphis, and arrived at Moses, Tennessee, at 2 P. M., an attack being anticipated on the small Union force at that place. We remained at Moses till the 10th, (the rest of the Division moving on to Lagrange, Tennessee ;) then we also moved on to that place. On the 13th, we took up our line of march, moving on toward Corinth, Mississippi, and arrived at that place on the 15th, at 8 P. M. The next day, we marched at 11 A. M., and that night we camped at Glendale Station ; on the 18th, we moved at 7 A. M., and arrived at Iuka at 5 P. M ; on the 19th, we moved at 4 A. M., and camped that night at Deer Creek. Next morning we moved at 6, and that day we arrived at Cherokee Station, in Alabama, and on the M. & C. R. R. There we remained till the 26th, and skirmishing was nearly all the time going on between the 1st Division of our Corps and the Rebel cavalry. On the morning of the 26th, we started at 4 A. M. for Tuscumbia, Alabama ; skirmishing was going on all day at the front. The next day the Rebels were driven from Tuscumbia, though they manifested considerable obstinacy ; and our Regiment was "under fire" during most of the day. The next day (the 28th,) we returned to Cherokee Station, and on the 29th our Regiment accompanied a "forage train" as guards, to a large valley of the Tennessee River, and returned to camp. On this occasion, a most melancholy accident occurred : Sergeant H. T. Cayton, of Co. A., was taken ill, and got into a wagon to ride to camp. The teamster drove rapidly, and Cayton's bayonet fell out of its sheath, and he fell on its point, and was thereby mortally wounded in the side. He died at Eastport, Tennessee, on the 3d of November.

On the 30th of October, we left for Eastport, on the Tennessee River, and marched all day through a heavy rain and deep mud, the Rebels following and skirmishing with our rear most of the day. These Rebels were under command of Roddy, Chalmers and Forrest. We arrived at Chickesaw, an old town, two miles above Eastport, at 10 P. M., on the 31st. At this place we received two months' pay. During the night of November 1st, and on the afternoon of the 2d, we crossed the Tennessee River, and camped at Waterloo, Mississippi. The next day we marched to Gravelly Springs, Alabama, and the night of the 4th we camped one mile east of Florence, Alabama, having passed through that old town in the afternoon. The night of the 5th we camped at Blue Creek. On this day, Sergeant Robert Love was promoted to 1st Lieutenant and Adjutant of the Regiment. On the 9th we passed through the once pretty town of Pulaski, Tennessee, and at night went into camp, two miles east of the town. On the 10th we passed through the still prettier town, Fayetteville, Tennessee, situated on Flint River, which has a splendid stone bridge, built of masonry, entire. It has six arches, and, of course, five piers and two abutments supporting it; we camped 8 miles east of this place that night. The next day, at about 2 P. M., we made a turn to the right, leaving the Winchester road, traveling toward Huntsville. We now found the great worth of such a man as our Surgeon, William Gillespie ; for he was now in charge of our Regiment, Dr. Davis having resigned at Camp Sherman, for he (Gillespie) was in the habit of talking to such as fell behind, on account of a want of strength to march up in the ranks, in such a style that they were sure to take courage, and if they continued to fail, he was sure to help them along in some way, if there was no room in the ambulances for them. About this time we were for two days passing through barren table lands, interspersed with sloughs and swamps.

On the 12th, we passed the little deserted town of New Market. The night of the 13th we camped near Maysville, at which place we saw General Wilder's Brigade. The next day we arrived near Scottsborough, Alabama. On the 16th we passed through Stevenson, where the M. & C. R. R. forms a junction; we camped that night 5 miles east of town. We arrived at Bridgeport on the 17th of November, and remained there till the 19th, on the morning of which we crossed the Tennessee River, and camped at night at Shell Mound; here we were met by some of our Indiana friends of the 35th Indiana Volunteers; here we saw Nickojack Cave, or one of its entrances, which is large enough to admit a four-horse team for some distance, and a stream of water issues from its mouth large enough to turn a good-sized mill. On the 20th we passed Whitesides. Here is the notorious John A. Murrell's Cave; at the entrance of this cave, there is still some of the masonry done by that arch-robber in fixing a doorway to the cave. On the 21st, we passed in full view of Lookout Mountain, and camped on the battlefield of Gen. Hooker, in the valley. On the 23d, we crossed the Tennessee River, in the valley, and rested till the afternoon of the 23d, and then, at 4 P. M., we moved to the river, 6 miles above Chattanooga, reaching it after dark, then lay down and awaited the boats (140 in number,) to come down out of a stream above, in which they had been launched during the day; at 2 A. M. of the 24th, the boats were ready for us ; we then effected a crossing in the most perfect silence possible, and the enemy was totally ignorant of our movements, and by daylight we had our whole Division intrenched, and were ready for action if we should be attacked, and we reasonably expected it, for the Rebels had, the night previous to our crossing, confronted the same place with artillery ; but Sherman's troops not making their appearance, they supposed it was not his intention to cross at that place. When we did cross, our General succeeded in capturing all the enemy's pickets, and by daylight all our Corps was well across the river, except the first Division, which, under Gen. Osterhaus, joined Gen. Hooker in the fight on Lookout Mountain the same day. At about noon we advanced in line of battle, and moved about six miles, and up the steep and long rise of Missionary Ridge, gaining its two Northwestern heights that afternoon, with but little fighting ; in fact the Rebels failed to reach the heights till we had them in our possession, though they made a strong effort to gain them first. The battle was now raging on Lookout Mountain with unmeasured fury, and continued to do so till after midnight ; this night Co. A. lay outside of the picket line, having skirmished all the afternoon, during which time it rained hard, and at night cleared off cold, so their position was not a very comfortable one ; the Regiment was also on less than half rations, and hunger, united with cold, made us feel that war was not a pleasant business, by any means. At 9 A. M. of the 25th, Co. A. was called in, and the 83d was chosen to support a Battery on Lightburn's Hill, as the second height of the Ridge was afterward called, in honor of his Brigade gaining it on the 24th. From this point we had a splendid view of nearly the whole extent of the line of the contending armies, from the point where we were to Lookout Mountain, probably 10 or 12 miles in extent. We felt hunger severely, but on the evening of the 26th we somewhat replenished our haversacks from the stores of the flying army of Bragg, which had so lately threatened to destroy or capture the Army of the Cumberland, now saved by the timely arrival of Gen. Sherman, with his well-tried army. We pursued the flying Rebels two days, and then received orders to go back and rebuild a bridge on the Chickamauga Creek, which the Rebels had destroyed on their retreat. We arrived at the spot on the morning of the 27th, and immediately set about the work, and at noon of the 3d of December, we had finished the bridge ; but we still remained there guarding the bridge till the 12th, meanwhile gathering some forage from the country near by, to help out our short rations ; we were also in need of some new clothes, the weather being frosty and cold for that part of the country.

We marched at 7 A. M. of the 13th, passed through Chattanooga, re-crossed the Tennessee River, and laid in an old camp 6 miles west of town that night, it being an extremely rainy, disagreeable time. Next day we were compelled to walk on the railroad ties, to keep out of the deep mud. We arrived near Shell Mound for that night, and camped, and on the afternoon of the 15th we arrived at Bridgeport, Alabama ; here we went into camp, and began putting up winter quarters, but learning that we must move further west, we desisted from building ; we spent Christmas, and were paid off for the months of September and October, and on the 26th left camp at 9 A. M., and moved to Bellefonte, where we arrived on the 29th, and again put up winter quarters, which we were destined soon to leave, as we had those at Bridgeport ; here we were two whole days without rations of any sort. This occurred by the carelessness of some functionary unknown to us. On New Years' Day, part of the Regiment accompanied a forage train out 8 miles into the country northward, and succeeded in getting something to stop the ravages of hunger. On the 7th of January, we moved to Larkinsville, Alabama, where we again put up winter quarters.

It is proper here to notice, that on this trip from Chattanooga to Larkinsville, our teams were not able to keep up with us, on account of the bad state of the roads, and, indeed, in going through the "narrows," between Whitesides and Shell Mound, some days they could not succeed in moving more than one half mile. They left many of their mules "dead and buried" in the mud.

We must also give a brief description of these "narrows." The road, for $1\frac{1}{2}$ miles, runs close on the steep bluff of the Tennessee River, 50 feet below, and the railroad passes along about 100 feet above the common road, and is, for the greater part of the way, built in a track made for it by art through the side of a mass of freestone, rising above on the south side, to the heighth of 200 feet. The same description will apply to the point of Lookout Mountain, only, in this latter case, the rock rises in still grander sublimity, and about midway of this precipice, and about 10 feet above the railroad track, is the entrance of a very extensive cave, which probably connects with those at Shell Mound, and the one whose entrance is near Ringgold. In this cave, on the point of Lookout Mountain, was found the remains of a woman, supposed to have been murdered by the Rebels while they occupied the mountains. She was found by some of the 5th Ohio Cavalry, and interred about 50 yards west of the mouth of the cave, and her grave marked, "A Victim of Rebel Cruelty." This the writer saw with his own eyes. But, we were destined to remain in our quiet and pleasant quarters at Larkinsville but a short time, for, on the 11th day of February, we marched again by way of Chattanooga to Cleveland, Tennessee. The Regiment was now under command of Lieut. Col. Myers, for Col. Spooner had gone home on leave of absence. We reached Bellefonte the day we marched. On the 12th we reached Bridgeport, and on the 13th arrived at Whitesides, and the next day we reached Chattanooga, and camped $\frac{1}{2}$ mile east of the foot of Lookout Mountain. On the 16th we moved to Ottawa ; then, on the 17th, we moved to Cleveland, Tennessee, a pleasant town, 30 miles from Chattanooga, on the Knoxville R. R. Here we spent about two weeks pleasantly for soldiers, while the other troops of the 15th Corps made a demonstration against Johnson's forces at Dalton, so as to favor Gen. Sherman in his "great raid" in Mississippi.

At 11 A. M., of March 1st, our Regiment marched on its return to Larkinsville. It rained all day hard, till 4 P. M., then cleared up cold ; we arrived and camped near Ottawa (18 miles) just at dark, and spent a very disagreeable night, having no axes to cut wood, and it being difficult to get anything dry to make fires of. On the 2d we arrived at Chattanooga, and on the 3d we reached Shell Mound ; and now it would be difficult to tell where we camped, or how we marched, for most of the men got on board of the train, and went on to camp at Larkinsville, as also did most of all other regiments ; but all had arrived safely at camp by the 6th, and were again in their old quarters. On this trip our Regiment was joined by Major Eggleston ; this was when we were at Cleveland.

We were all glad to be again pleasantly in camp to rest, and to exchange letters with our friends at the North, from whom we had now been absent for about 19 months, and many of us received articles of clothing and sanitaries from our homes in Indiana. This gave us great pleasure, to hold communication with our loved ones at home.

Col. Spooner was also welcomed back to camp on the 19th of March, and was soon after presented with a fine sword, box and belt, costing $350, by the privates and non-commissioned officers of the Regiment. Upon the receipt of this present he thanked them in an eloquent speech, recounting all our victories and hardships, reminding us that our time had not yet expired, and we had a history of noble deeds yet to finish.

The scenery around the valley of Larkinsville was fine. The large hills and mountains rising in sight at every point of the compass; one might count 20 of their tops from a single stand point; the timber, of pine, oak, hickory, cedar, &c., intermingling and rising in majestic grandeur in those fertile valleys and caves, are intermingled with magnificent heights and beautiful streams that flow through all the valleys of East Tennessee.

For the most part of the time of our stay at Larkinsville, the weather was fine and pleasant, but on the night of March 21st, snow fell to the depth of near a foot, and the weather was cold; this was the deepest snow that we ever encountered during all the time of our service in the army. However, we had good quarters and plenty in the line of clothing and rations, so we passed the time comfortably as well as pleasantly. We also received pay from the Government up to December 31st, and also had an opportunity to send our money home to our friends and families, by the hand of a citizen of Dearborn Co. (Mr. Miller,) and it all reached our homes in safety. Indeed, it was a treat to receive a visit from such an old friend and patriot as Mr. Miller.

One more item of history relative to our stay at Larkinsville we must note: The interest felt by the 83d in the political campaign which came off the following Fall, was intense. They had regained all their former stamina in a political sense now almost to a man ; they indorsed all the measures of the President to put down the Rebellion, and especially they desired the re-election of the noble Governor of Indiana ; and feeling that they had been greatly swindled and wronged by that party that had succeeded in procuring legislation against soldiers voting in the field, they, on the 12th day of April, held a meeting and drew up a manifesto, expressing their loyalty and adherence to the Union, the Constitution, and a vigorous prosecution of the war, and the indignation they felt at being deprived of the privilege of an approach to the ballot-box by those sham friends of the Constitution, but real friends of the "Southern Confederacy," nearly every man subscribed to the manifesto, and the same was published in the Versailles Dispatch of May 5th, 1864. The number of officers and men who signed it was 303, of whom 21 were officers, including all the Field and Staff. There were a few who were off on detail and on detached duty, that would have signed the manifesto if they had been present, among whom was the writer.

CHAPTER V.

And now it became necessary for us to begin thinking about another campaign. Spring was close at hand, and the Rebel army, under Gen. Joseph E. Johnson, was at and around Dalton, Ga., only a little more than 100 miles from us, intending to resist all efforts of our army to re-establish the authority of the United States in all the seceded States. But, "the God of Eternal Rule," by means of Gen. Sherman and his "Bonny Boys in Blue," must decide in the case. And here I think it in place to introduce some few lines, written by one of Sherman's boys, while incarcerated in a Rebel prison:

"SHERMAN'S MARCH TO THE SEA."

Our camp fires shone bright on the mountain,
    That frowned on the river below,
When we stood by our guns in the morning,
    And eagerly watched for the foe;
When a rider came out from the darkness,
    That hung over mountain and tree,
And shouted, "Boys, up and be ready,
    For Sherman will march to the sea."

Then, cheer upon cheer for bold Sherman,
    Went up from each valley and glen,
And the bugles re-echoed the music,
    That came from the lips of the men;
For, we knew that the stars in our banner
    More bright in their splendor would be,

And blessings from North-land would greet us,
　　When Sherman marched down to the sea.

Then forward, boys, forward to battle,
　　We marched on our wearisome way,
And we stormed the wild hills of Resaca,
　　God bless those who fell on that day!
Then, Kenesaw, dark in its glory,
　　Frowned down on the Flag of the Free;
But the East and West bore our standard,
　　And Sherman marched on to the sea.

Still onward we pressed, till our banner
　　Swept out from Atlanta's grim walls,
And the blood of the patriot dampened
　　The soil where the traitor flag falls.
But, we pause not to weep for the fallen,
　　Who sleep by each river tree;
Yet we twined them a wreath of the laurel
　　As Sherman marched down to the sea.

Proud, proud was our army that morning,
　　That stood where the pine darkly towers,
And Sherman said, "Boys, your'e weary;
　　This day, fair Savannah is ours!"
Then, sang we a song for our chieftain,
　　That echoed o'er river and lea,
And the stars in our banner shone brighter,
　　For Sherman had marched to the sea.

On the 28th of April, we received orders to be ready to march at a moments notice, "with entire camp and garrison equippage," but did not march till the morning of the 1st of May, when we moved by the way of Bridgeport and Chattanooga, thence up the Chattanooga Valley, thence we passed the old Chickamauga battle ground, on the afternoon of the 6th, and camped near the upper extent of the battle field. The next morning we crossed the Chickamauga Creek at a large mill, and pushed on. On the 7th we crossed "Taylor's Ridge," and on the 8th we passed through "Snake Creek Gap," a narrow pass six miles long, through "Horn's Mountains." Having gained possession of this "pass," it was fortified on the 9th, and the 83d was stationed at the cross-roads, two miles in advance of the entrance of the Gap. They were supported by artillery, and an abundance of help lay at hand in case the rebels saw fit to come out from Ressaca, only seven miles distant, and attack our forces. But they did not do so. The night of the 9th was a terribly stormy one; the rain descended in torrents, and it was difficult to "keep our powder dry."

On the morning of May 13th we moved on the Rebels at Resaca, and fell in with their skirmishers two miles from town, and drove them into their works. On the 14th we charged them and took possession of a hill, or rather a ridge, extending parallel with their works, which we fortified and held. Soon after we got possession of this position and got it fortified, or rather a line of earthworks thrown up to protect us, the enemy charged us, and were repulsed with severe loss. This was in the afternoon, about three o'clock. But the hardest fighting on this occasion took place on the afternoon of the 14th, when "we charged the wild hills of Resaca." The writer, (being with the Division Pioneers all this summer,) stood on one of those hills about one and a-half miles to the west of Ressaca, and where one of our batteries was engaged behind a redoubt, playing on one of the enemy's forts, to the left of the town. Here we had a plain view of all the valley, which was now the scene of bloody conflict. Musket balls were flying like hail in all directions, and shells were bursting, and "grape and cannister was whistling over the wide-spread scene." "The cannon's deep roar," the flash and smoke of artillery, and bursting shells from both sides, rendered the scene lively and vivid in the extreme. Thus it continued, till dark put an end to the bloody strife. But during the day and night of the 15th the rebels evacuated all their works from Rocky Face to Ressaca. So on the morning of the 16th, General Sherman set his army in motion to pursue the retreating enemy.

We should have stated that we left Dr. Wm. Gillespie very sick, at Larkinsville, and he was never afterwards able to accompany the Regiment. This we greatly regretted, for there were few that could fill the place with so much acceptance to the Regiment. Dr. Keller, of the 6th Missouri Volunteers, accompanied the 83d on the spring campaign up to the time we went into camp at Eastport, Georgia.

These digressions will enable us to avoid reference to those things another time.

The 15th Corps being on the extreme right, it became necessary for us to cross the Saluda River, some six or eight miles below the scenes of the few days. We effected this crossing on the 16th, before dark, by means of two pontoon bridges, and went into camp for the night about a mile from the river. We reached Kingston, where the railroad forks, one branch going to Rome, Ga., and the other, or main road, going on toward Atlanta, on the 20th, about 2 P. M., and camped on the Etowan River for the time being, the weather being extremely hot. On the morning of the 23d we moved early, and crossed the above-named river at the lower one of two bridges which our cavalry had secured. This was at a plantation belonging to Alexander H. Stevens, once the Vice-President of the "Southern Confederacy." We reached Dallas by a circuitous route through Van Wert, Paulding county, Georgia, on the 26th, and began skirmishing with the enemy, occupying a range of hills near Dallas, (in the same county above named,) their right resting near the town. This range is called " Winding Ridge," and afforded a strong position for resisting an advancing force.

On the 27th we built works in our front, under the fire of the enemy. Skirmishing continued sharply all day, and the next day was continued till 5 P. M., when the rebels charged us in our works, and, of course, were repulsed with heavy loss. Our loss was ten men killed and wounded. On the morning of the 29th of May, at about 7 o'clock, a most melancholy occurrence took place. Lieutenant Colonel Benjamin H. Myers exposed himself by going over in front of our works, and was unfortunately shot dead by the enemy.

Skirmishing continued all day of the 30th, and and on the 31st we moved a little to the left, where the 20th Corps had been fighting, and held the lines till the rebels withdrew, on the night of the 4th of June, and, on the 6th, we arrived at Ackworth, (a nice little town on the railroad,) about noon, at which place we camped till the morning of the 10th, and that day we moved to Big Shanty, and found the enemy occupying Kennesaw Mountains, which are about four miles south of Big Shanty Station.

Here we were confronted by the enemy for more than three weeks. Up to the 27th of June we were engaged day and night, with but little rest, in fortifying and advancing our lines, and in skirmishing and sharpshooting. On this day our division and other parts of the army made an assault on "Little Kenesaw," where the rebels occupied strong works, and also having a "cross-fire" on us with a large amount of Artillery. The steeps of the mountain slopes were so rough and encumbered with huge rocks, that we found it impossible to ascend far up under such a gauling fire as they continued to pour into us. We gained some of their rifle pits, and did not fall back to our original position, but having gained an advanced position, we fortified it, and held the rebels back where we had forced them to.

But our loss in this bloody charge was heavy, having lost our Colonel, who was severely wounded in the left arm, and which had to be amputated at the shoulder next day, we also lost ten men killed and wounded.

The scene of this days fight beggars all description. The ground all around the mountains is exceedingly rough, deep ravines, steep hills, sloughs, open fields and thickets are intermingled together in indiscribable confusion. Over such and all of these we had to charge, so that it was difficult to tell our position, or see from what quarter danger threatened us most. Sometimes the missiles of death were showered upon us, and seemed to come down from over our heads, and shells would strike and plow up the ground, covering us with dirt and bursting in the earth would kill or wound some and hoist others from a chosen position. These things, mingled with the cries of the wounded and dying of both armies, made the scene terrible. The rebels fought desperately, but as they lay wounded and helpless in the excessive heat, they would call out, "Oh, good Yankees, give me some water!" Thus passed the 27th of June, 1864, winding up from sunrise till dark with a terrific canonading from both side. This was at the south-west side of "Little Kenesaw."

Sometimes during this three weeks seige, the rebels after a long silence would open on us with several guns from the top of the mountain, but in less than a minute, you might see the flash of a dozen shells thrown from our cannon, and bursting almost at once, just at the point where a moment before rose the flash and smoke of the enemies guns. This in the distant twilight resembled a host of lightening-bugs displaying their illuminating qualities.

On the 2d day of July we moved to the extreme right of the army. On the 4th we advanced and drove the flank of the enemy, and that night they fell back to the Chattahochee river, where they had another line of strong works. On the 7th we took position on the east side of the Sand Town road, and fortified our position. By the morning of the 10th the rebels had crossed to the south side of the river, and on the 11th we moved to the extreme right again to relieve some cavalry. At 5 P. M. of the 12th, we moved toward the left, and next morning we passed through Marietta, a nice town, three miles south of the Kenesaw mountains, on our way to Rosswell, another nice town, twelve miles east of the former named place, and situated on the hills of Nickojack Creek, on which at the distance of three miles from the Chattahoochee river, Rosswell King and a Mr. Dunwoody, both from the State of Connecticut, built an extensive wool and cotton cloth factory; but our army destroyed it all by fire as soon as they reached it, the proprietors being rank secessionists. On the 14th we crossed the Chattahoochee river at the mouth of Neckojack Creek, at 5 P. M., our division taking a position on the heights east of the river, where we built strong works. We moved on the morning of the 17th in the direction of Stone mountain, arriving at the Augusta and Atlanta railroad at 5 P. M. on the 18th, when we began destroying it, and the next day we followed it up, destroying it as we went along, until we arrived at Decatur, when we took possession of that town and camped for the night. On the 20th we moved toward Atlanta, skirmishing with the rebels as we went until within a short distance of the city. The next day we built works, and on the 22d a severe battle ensued, but fortunately the 83d was in the rear that day guarding the hospital and the ambulance train, and so escaped the fight. On the 24th our Regiment was sent in charge of about 1,200 prisoners to Marietta, and returned on the 26th.

On the 27th, we moved to the extreme right of the army; a hard days march.

On the 28th we advanced and got into position on the "line of battle," about 10 A. M., but before we had time to construct works to any extent, the enemy charged upon us in heavy force, six or eight lines deep; but we stood our ground, and succeeded in repulsing them with a heavy slaughter, and we also took many prisoners. Our Regiment lost in this battle 19 men killed, wounded and captured. It was a most terrific affair. Our division fired 34,300 rounds of cartridges in the fight, in the small space of four hours. Artillery could not be used by our men in this fight. We now fortified our position and remained on the same part of the line until the 27th of August, often making demonstrations to favor other parts of the army, and often advancing our lines.

On the evening of the 27th of August, we left the front at 8 o'clock, and marching all night we reached the West Point railroad at 3 P. M. of the 28th, and having destroyed it effectually, we moved forward on the 30th, skirmishing all day. We reached the Macon and Atlanta Railroad, near Jonesborough, and here we built works on the forenoon of the 31st, and at 3 P. M. the rebels charged on us in our works, and were again repulsed with heavy loss. Indeed they stated that they were whipped worst here than they had been in all the campaign.

On the 2d of September, we entered Jonesborough, the rebels having withdrawn to Lovejoy Station, and evacuated Atlanta. On the 6th of September we started back toward Atlanta, and arrived at Eastport, Ga., on the 8th, having marched 425 miles during the campaign that had now lasted for more than four months, and our Regiment had been in five heavy battles and many skirmishes.

One thing we should notice here, is, that the country through which we moved on this campaign is one of the healthiest parts of the South, and is well watered with the best of springs of the crystal fluid issuing from the sides of the hills and mountains, that present a very picturesque appearance to the passing observer. If this had not been the case, it is extremely doubtful whether either army could have endured the exposures, toils and hard fighting on this campaign, now ending so successful to our cause.

Though we went into regular camp at Eastport, the junction of the Westpoint, Atlanta & Macon railroads, six miles south of Atlanta, we remained there nearly a month, yet we did not have such a time of rest and recuperation as we had before enjoyed at Camp Sherman, and at Larkinsville, for our rations were short and our time was taken up in drilling and in working on fortifications, and the weather being very warm, and most of the time raining, so that our stay here was not so agreeable as it would have been if we had been surrounded by more favorable circumstances.

Many of the boys strongly believed, (or hoped) that our Regiment would be called home to Indiana, to enjoy the privilege of attending the State and Presidential elections, and all were anxious to cast a vote for the re-election of the Governor of our State, who had always shown such an interest in the health of Indiana soldiers, as well as in the success of our arms, and in sustaining the General Government in the great struggle against armed treason. But on the 4th day of October we were again on the move after Hood's army, which had got in the rear of General Sherman's army, in order to cut our communication and force us to fall back into Kentucky.

For some time our marching was moderate. On the 6th we passed through Marietta, Ga., and remained in the vicinity of Kenesaw Mountains until the evening of the 12th, and then moved at 4 P. M., and marching day and night, we arrived at Ressaca at 8 A. M. of the 15th, direct by way of Altoona, Cartersville and Kingston. At sunset of the 15th, we entered "Snake Creek Gap," the 17th Corps in our front skirmishing with the "rear guard" of one part of Hood's army. The rebels had piled the road through the pass full of trees, felling them in from both sides, and it was near the middle of the night, dark and raining, when we got through the gap, and obtained a short time for rest and sleep, until the morning. On the 17th we reached Lafayette, the rebels having turned their course towards Huntsville, Ala. On the next day we marched to Summerville, Ga., and on the night of the 19th, we camped at Belmont. On the 20th we made 22 miles, and camped that night at Galesville, Ala. On the 21st we moved 7 miles, to Little River, and the next day the 83d accompanied the wagon train to Rome, Ga., as guards, and arrived there at 4 P. M. of the 23d, the distance we made there in two days was 33 miles.

On the 24th we moved back 25 miles toward Little river, and joined the division on the 25th, at the same place where we had left it on the 22d, and where we remained till the 29th, when we crossed the Coosey river, heading southward again at 5 P. M., and marched till late that night. On the 31st about 10 A. M., we arrived at Cave city, or Cave Springs, as it was formerly called, we stopped here to be mustered, and the next day we reached Cedar Town and camped at 2 P. M. On the 1st of November we moved to Powder Springs, and on the 5th we reached Rough Station, near the Chattahochee river, after a march of 350 miles, where we remained till the 10th, passing a very rainy and disagreeable time. This time was spent in fitting out for a fall campaign, or a renewal of the same one in which we had been engaged all the season, and here we got eighth months' pay on the 9th of November, 1864.

CHAPTER VI.

On the 10th of Nov. we moved ten miles by a circuitous route to the pontoon bridge across the river, and remained there as guards till the 14th, while the troops were crossing; and on the afternoon of the 14th we crossed over and drew some new clothing, and that night marched to the east side of the conquered city of Atlanta, and on the morning of the 15th we started at 8 A. M., on our "long and tedious march" to Savannah, leaving that once central flourishing city in flames. The smoke could be seen for many miles. Our route layed eastwardly; and having marched 18 miles, we camped for the night, an hour after dark.

On the 16th we made 16 miles to Madisonville. The next day we moved 15 miles, and on the 18th we made only 12 miles to a town called Indian Springs, 8 miles from the Ocmulgee river. On the morning of the 19th we moved at 6 o'clock, and at 12 we crossed the above-named river on two pontoon bridges, and after marching all day through the rain and mud, we went into camp, having made 16 miles. On the 20th we only marched 12 or 14 miles, and did not get into camp till 9 P. M., the rain still coming down on us, and making traveling very laborious. This night's march many will long recollect, for nearly every man on foot, both officers and soldiers, fell down, some of them a dozen times.

On the 21st we made 13 miles, the rain still coming in torrents all night, and continuing till 3 P. M. of this day. On this day at 10 A. M., we passed the place where Stoneman was captured by the rebels in July, 1864, and the same day we passed through the town of Clinton. The country in this vicinity is a little hilly and more fertile than most of that we had seen in Georgia. On the 22d we crossed the railroad leading from Augusta to Macon, and within 6 miles of the latter city. On the afternoon of this day, the rebels made a charge on Gen. Walcott's brigade of the 1st Division of the 15th Corps, and were repulsed with heavy loss. This took place at Griswoodville, 8 miles from Macon. Near this place, (about 11 A. M.) Joseph H. Gillman of company F, and August Bush of company A, were attacked as they were foraging, by some twenty or thirty rebels. Gillman was killed on the spot, but Bush made his escape by dodging into the corners of a fence along which he ran, till out of the reach of their fire. This was now a cold time, and a slight snow fell during the night of the 21st, and the 22d was windy and cold as at the city of Cincinnati in common winter weather, and ice froze that night to the thickness of near an inch.

On the 23d we moved 9 miles, camped at 2 P. M., and put up earthworks. On the 24th we moved 12 miles, and camped at 3 P. M., in sight of Erwintown, and again put up works. On the 25th we reached the Oconee river, the advance skirmishing with the rebels. After dark, on the evening of the 26th we crossed the Oconee on a pontoon bridge, and camped 4 miles from the crossing.

On the 27th we moved only 10 miles; the country now beginning to be more swampy, though slightly rolling, it is also interspersed with many sloughs, grown up with sweet gum, cypress and many other sorts of shrubs, though the high land is here wooded with a fine growth of tall pitch pine. All along through this part of the country we found an abundance of the finest sweet potatoes, and also " fresh hog and bacon," in abundance.

On the 29th we made a hard march of 20 miles, for we had to march out of the road over logs, &c., and the pine shacks and dry grass made it so slippery that it was tiresome in the extreme. The reason of our going out of the road was to give the train a chance to be just with us and so be in perfect safety. This way of marching was continued during all this and on subsequent campaigns through South and North Carolina. On the 30th we made 18 miles, and camped at Summerville. On the 1st of Dec. we moved 16 miles, and on the 2d we made 12 miles, and on the morning of the 3d we moved 2 miles and waded a deep, cold swamp then halted and built works, and remained till the next day, while the pioneers were engaged in corduroying the roads so as to enable the trains and artillery to get along.

On the 4th we moved 15 miles, and that night camped at Statesborough, where the advance of our column, being on the extreme right of the army, had a sharp skirmish with a regiment of Mississippi rebel cavalry, that happened to be there at that time, on its way northward. But they left in a hurry, leaving several of their number dead on the spot, but succeeded in taking some of our "bummers" prisoners. Each regiment of Sherman's army had a number of men detailed and mounted, whose business it was to ride over the country in the advance, and gather in forage and eatables, and these were vulgarly called "bummers." This arrangement was kept up till we reached Raleigh, North Carolina. They were much exposed, and many of them taken, and in some instances they were killed by the lawless guerrillas after they had taken them prisoners, and left unburied in those wild pine forests of Georgia.

On the 5th of Dec. we moved 14 miles, and on the 6th we moved 3 miles and fortified. On the 7th we marched 15 miles. This was another rainy day.

Here the writer claims the privilege of narrating a little incident. as an illustration of an overruling and controlling Providence. Being on picket 1 1-2 miles from camp, it was my turn to go on the vedette post at 11 o'clock; but about ten minutes before my time, we heard the center on the vedette, shout "halt! halt!" and instantly fired on two rebels who had come out into the road, 75 yards in his front, and made of into the woods again. I went out at the proper time, with another man, and as we were giving the instructions to our "relief," I saw five men coming by the same road, on which two hours and a half before, those two rebels had been fired at by my predecessor. I said, "there they come, boys," and springing across the road, I snapped my gun at them twice, and one of my comrades shot at them. "Who's there?" shouted they. "The 15th Corps," said I, "Good for you," said one; "we belong to it too." "Well, said I, if you do, you know the rules, you will dismount, and come one at a time." They obeyed, and when the Lieutenant in charge came up he told me that my partner's ball burned his face as it passed, and that they all snapped their carbines at us, and that in a moment more they would have charged upon us, for they were scouts, taking orders to our division head-quarters, and must go through. It seems providential, indeed, that so many pieces were snapped, but only one shot was fired and all our lives were saved.

On the morning of the 8th, we crossed Black Creek, and marched 16 miles that day, passing Eden Court House, where, the day previous to our arrival, the 4th Division of the 15th Corps had a sharp skirmish with the enemy. We camped near the Canoochee River that night; the next morning, at 2 o'clock, we were aroused by a volley of musketry and several cannon shots. The Rebels occupied some works on the opposite bank of the river, and were trying to prevent the "Yanks" from getting possession of the crossing; for they had destroyed the main part of the bridge, and were firing the remainder with lighted faggots, but a few shots were sufficient to dislodge them, and by noon the next day, the bridge was so repaired that we all crossed the river, and by 3 P. M. (of the 9th) we reached the Gulf Railroad, 6 miles from the river, and our Brigade destroyed 6 miles of the Road, and returned and went into camp by the river at the late hour of 10 o'clock. On the morning of December 10th, we re-crossed the Canoochee, and made a circuit and crossed it again farther up, and proceeding, we crossed the Big Ogeechee River and camped, after having made 12 miles. We were now in supporting distance of the front, or "in reserve," as is commonly said, until the evening of the 12th, when we moved four miles back, to King's Bridge, but could not cross, for the bridge was not quite repaired. The next morning we proceeded across, and making a circuitous route down the river, we got within two miles of Fort McAllister at half-past 10 A. M., and "stacked arms." Three regiments of each Brigade (nine regiments) moved on and formed in line, one mile from the fort, charged and took it by storm ; but the 83d lay "in reserve," and did not participate in this brilliant affair.

Fort McAllister was a strong work, containing 24 guns, on the south bank of the Big Ogeechee, and had resisted successfully all the efforts of the gunboats to take it. It was commanded by one Major Anderson, and was garrisoned by only about 300 men, but they fought desperately till overpowered by our men, actually in the Fort. The Union loss was about 40 in killed and wounded.

The taking of this Fort opened the "cracker line" for Sherman's whole army, which was now short of rations; and well they might be, for they had been without communication with home and the whole North for an entire month.

We remained near this fort till near noon of the 17th, then moved 14 miles and camped for the night, hungry and tired, for we had no rations with us, and did not get any for two days, except a very short supply of forage. We started early the next morning, and arrived at McIntosh Station, on the Gulf Railroad, 30 miles from Savannah, at 12 M., having made 12 miles, and were there engaged in destroying the road, burning every tie and twisting every rail, till the evening of the 20th. On the morning of the 21st we started back, and again crossed the Big Ogeechee, at King's Bridge, and went into camp an hour after dark, among the dead pines, in an old corn-field, having made 22 miles that day. We heard that night that the Rebels had evacuated Savannah. On the 22d we moved 3 miles, and camped 12 miles from Savannah till the 29th, and then moved to within 4 miles of the city, and stopped in camp till the 2d of January, 1865, when we moved at 10 A. M. and went into camp at the suburbs of the city, or rather in the old fortifications of this old city, founded in 1673, by General Oglethorpe. It is situated on the south bank of the Savannah River, 18 miles above its mouth, where it joins Ossaban Sound. It is a great place for fish and oysters; presents a healthful appearance, though not as beautiful as many other cities of its size, and is an important maritime port. It is noted as the place of General Pulaski's monument, who was mortally wounded at the seige of Savannah, in 1792. The city has a harbor sufficient for all its mercantile capacities, allowing vessels of medium tonnage to ascend at "high tide" to the city docks.

On the 9th of January we moved into the city, and camped near the city docks, put up quarters on a vacant square, and were on duty at the wharf till the 15th, when we were relieved, having orders to march at 5 A. M.

It is proper to state that the 83d, on this long march, had been accompanied by two surgeons, Dr. Cornelius B. Coe, of the 29th Missouri Volunteers, and Dr. John C. Morgan, of the same regiment, the former of whom was one of the most popular surgeons that ever attended to the wants of sick men in our Regiment. We were now also without any Chaplain since the 1st of October, 1864, both of our Chaplains having resigned and left us to the fate which might overtake us.

CHAPTER VII.

On the morning of the 15th of January, moved to Fort Thunderbolt, five miles down the Savannah river, and remained there till the 16th, then at 9 A. M. got on board of a vessel, (the Delaware,) and at sunset the same evening, arrived at Beaufort, South Carolina, having descried Fort Pulaski far to our left as we entered the bay, and passing Hilton Head to our left, and Port Royal to our right, as we passed up the sound to Beaufort. But we could not disembark, till about midnight, on account of the tide being low, and so the vessel could not land at the dock till it rose. At 1 A. M. of the 17th we got off the boat and moved through the town, and lay down at the back part of it till daylight, for we could find neither wood to make fires, or a guide to show us to camp. The next morning we moved out 2 miles and went into camp to wait for the main part of the army to arrive, before we should start off on the campaign through the Carolinas. We remained here till the 27th, enjoying the fruit of the extensive oyster beds, so abundant in the sound.

On the 27th we moved 7 miles and went into camp till the 27th, having "general reviews" on the 28th, before taking a tramp through the "Old Traitor State," the home of the "nullifiers" of

1832. The command of the regiment now fell upon Capt. Wm. J. Craw, of Company I, for Lieut.-Col. Scott was compelled to remain behind on ac- of illness, and all the sick and those not able to march were also left at Beaufort.

So, on the morning of the 29th of January, we started at daylight, and passed Fort Pocataligo at 2 P. M., and arrived at Pocataligo Station, on the Charleston and Savannah R. R., at 4 P. M., where we remained till the morning of the 31st. As we were coming near to camp here, and passing our Division Headquarters, General Hazen stood looking at the men passing him, with their knapsacks full, and five days' rations in their haversacks, one of our Regiment said to him: "General, we are drawing 9 feet water!" The General laughed.

We marched at 5 A. M. of the 31st, and made 16 miles in nearly a western direction, and camped for the night. February 1st we marched 12 miles, and the next day we marched 18 miles, and then went out two miles farther with the 111th Illinois Volunteers, and built works. The next morning we were relieved, and returned to our Division at 10 A. M. Our foragers had a skirmish with some cavalry at a mill only a short distance off, and drove them away, taking sixty sacks of meal, that served us a good purpose, to camp with us. There was considerable skirmishing going on all the forenoon of the 2d.

Up to this time, our course had been nearly westward up the river toward Augusta, Ga., probably for the purpose of drawing the enemy to that place; and in this our Great Leader was successful. But now we turned nearly northward. The country was also very level and swampy, and the season being very rainy, it became necessary to corduroy the roads nearly all the way, else the train of wagons and the artillery could not get along, for the wheels would go right down to the hubs, and progress would be impossible. We marched 13 miles on the 4th, and on the 5th we made 16 miles. As we were going into camp this day, just at sunset, we heard a volley of nearly a dozen muskets at a half mile's distance; it was an attack made by some guerrillas on an ambulance and three men going out for some forage near by. Sergeant Peter Kruett, of Company F., was wounded in the hand, and one of the guerrillas was killed, and also one of the ambulance horses, but the enemy made their escape with the other horse.

On the 6th we marched 7 miles, crossing the Augusta and Charleston R. R. at Bamenburg, or Midway, as some call it. We stopped in camp about one mile north of the town till the next day, while most of the army was engaged in tearing up and destroying the road. On the 7th and 8th, we made 10 miles each day; the country through which we were now passing was level, fertile and thickly settled, but as the army passed, it was left in a desolate condition. Indeed, some days the sun was almost entirely obscured by the smoke of the consuming buildings, cotton gins, &c., and a citizen told me, after we had crossed the line in North Carolina, that Sherman's army had left a lane 80 miles wide through South Carolina entirely devastated. On the 9th we moved 8 miles, to the South Edisto River, and the 1st Brigade of our Division waded up to their knees and skirmished with the Rebels, who held some works on the north side of the stream, or rather running swamp, for it was about two miles wide, and also the 17th Corps was coming up on the enemy's flank, having crossed above, so they left in the night; on the 10th we crossed and moved 4 miles and built works, and on the 11th we moved 13 miles, and again built works. February 12th, in the morning, we moved 3 miles to the North Edisto River; but here again the enemy held the north side of the river with fortifications, and it came the turn of our Brigade to drive them away, or take and destroy these flying Rebels, who were trying only to obstruct and impede our progress. This was no small undertaking, for they had burned the bridge over the stream at the road, and held the levee (the road) with a raking fire. The 83d Indiana and the 37th, 47th and 54th Ohio Regiments were sent above to flank the enemy. The river overflowed its banks to the distance of near a mile on each side of the main channel, which was not fordable, so all had to wade for about two miles to the depth of three feet in water extremely cold, crossing the channel by means of trees felled for the purpose, and they were in the water at least three hours. Sometimes men could be seen getting on a log or a stump, or climbing some leaning sapling to save themselves, so as to straighten their cramping limbs, and the Colonel of the 37th Ohio was often heard to soliloquize, "Oh, mein Gott, what is to become of us now." Our men formed their lines in the water, and advanced on the Rebels and routed them, taking 60 prisoners, without the loss of a man. We moved after the flying Rebels about 2 miles and threw up light works, and after dark we moved 3 miles to the east, halted and lay down till morning. The next day we made 15 miles, being train guards that day; we also turned north-westwardly, heading toward Columbia, having the Charleston and Columbia Railroad to our right. February 14th we marched 13 miles, and on the 15th we moved about 8 miles, the first Division of the 15th Corps skirmishing and driving the Rebels before them all day on our front. The mud was very bad in a large valley through which we traveled most of this day, for the Rebels had flooded it only two nights previously, by cutting some dams on a stream running through the valley. About dusk we came up with the 1st Division, and formed "in line" on their right, next to the Congaree River. The Rebels occupied a ridge, extending back at right angles from the river, and only a mile in our front. On this ridge they had strong works, and our artillery was playing on them at long range as we came in line at dark. We "pitched tents" and built our camp fires in full view of those of the enemy, only a mile in our front. Here was presented to the beholder a most splendid, as well as a most daring view of affairs. Tens of thousands of fires in this large valley invited the play of the enemy's masked batteries, if they should have such, and the probability was strong, for the notorious

Beauregard was in command. Well, we immediately set about putting up works, and soon found need of them, for about 8 o'clock, as we were contemplating the probability of a few "visitors," suddenly a flash to our right and a shell came plunging into the camp of the 48th Illinois Regiment, and now another, and another, killing a Lieutenant. These shells continued coming into various parts of the camp of the 15th Corps all night, from a battery across the river, till near daylight, then ceased for a little time, and then opened on us again, and continued to annoy our trains all day. But the 53d Ohio volunteers deployed along the bank of the river, and opened as sharpshooters on the Rebels, with such effect that their gunners could not load or fire their guns without being shot down, and Captain De Grass double-quicked part of his battery of 20-pounder Parrott guns, past the enemy's guns to a fort in our front, now abandoned by the Rebels, for they had left their position in our front on the ridge, and had crossed the river into the city of Columbia.

At 3 A. M. of the 15th, our skirmishers followed the rebels, but they burned the bridge across the Congaree, and so they could not follow. But our batteries were soon in position on the hill in front of the city, and it received a warm shelling, remunerative of the manner in which they had so foolishly tormented us the previous evening. The rebels had also burned the bridges on the Saluda and Broad rivers, which two forms the Congaree just at the upper edge of the city, but by 3 P. M., of the 15th, the pontoons were laid on the former, and we crossed and camped between the Soluda and Broad river, and on the afternoon of the 17th we crossed the last named river and marched through the city to the east side of it, and went into camp, for the rebels had evacuated and gone to Columbia, (where secession first took form) as seen from those heights, on the south side of the Congaree, presenting one of the most picturesque and beautiful views we had ever beheld. The city occupied a rise of half a mile, back from the river to the top of the hill, then extending back on the level for a mile and a half, and all extending east and west, up and down the river for three miles. The situation is high and slightly rolling, a most beautiful one; and the city was well laid off and substantially built. The State House had been in process of erection for ten years, the walls being four feet thick, of solid granite, a 20-pound shell thrown from a Parrot gun, at the distance of three-fourths of a mile, made no impression, but bounded back and bursted at a distance of fifty yards.

This building is slightly injured by the action of the fire that consumed all the combustibles in and about it. Our men were left pretty much with out orders in camp, on the night of the 17th, and feeling a disposition to visit the wealthy city, many of them went to town that night, and helped themselves to all they wished. Wines, whisky, tobacco, meat flour, meal, and in fact every article they fancied that they had need for, they took in abundance, so they "did eat and drink, and had a merry time generally," and by morning the one-half of the most solid built part of the city lay in ashes, and at daylight hundreds of women that had once given the greatest encouragement to the rebellion, might have been seen in omnibuses at the outskirts of the ruined city, looking at the "Yanks," now in the best of "spirits," and three days later there could not be any of this wealthy city seen, except a few of the "suburbs." The 18th and 19th was taken up in destroying the Charleston and Columbia railroad out for 30 miles; the 83d was out 15 miles and returned on the afternoon of the 19th. All this time had been taken up in blowing up the amunition and burning the cotton, and destroying all manner of public property, such as locomotives (25 of which were ruined) and rolling stock, etc. There was an immense amount of powder, and the reports of it, in blowing up, resembled thunder for two days and nights.

On the 20th of February we started on with the entire army of Sherman, and proceeded northward, and after marching 18 miles and wading a swamp "knee deep," we went into camp for the night. On the 21st we proceed 17 miles, and on the 22d we made 10 miles and halted for three hours at the Wateree river, till the pontoons were extended across the channel, and we crossed and went into camp 3 miles from the crossing, and 2 miles from Liberty Hill, an old town of Revolutionary note. On the 23d we passed through the town above-named, and made about 18 miles, passing Camden to our right, and went into camp 7 miles north of the town, at the late hour of 10 o'clock, it being a dark and rainy night. Along all this part of the South, nearly all the pines of those extensive forests are tapped to obtain turpentine and resin, as is also the case through North Carolina, and we found no trouble in lighting fires by splinters obtained from these trees, and by using the pine knots so abundant all along our route. Our faces and clothes became very sable in appearance, and it has been ironically said, that "one great reason why it seemed so late whenever we got into camp of nights, and daylight was so long in coming of mornings, was because our faces were so dark by this pine smoke!" The amount of resin found at many of these places would astonish one not used to see such countries. Sometimes hundreds of barrels of it would be found at one place, and never failed to make a "big smoke," for the "Yanks" left nothing in their wake. Hundreds of wagons, buggies and carriages were brought into camp of evenings by the foragers, laden with eatables, and in the morning the boys would pile them on the fire and leave them burning; indeed they felt no disposition to favor these inveterate Rebels of South Carolina.

February 24th, we marched 20 miles, and on the 25th made 8 miles, and had a terrific thunder storm in the evening. On the 26th we moved 10 miles and waded Lynch Creek three feet deep, (for 200 yards) and half a mile wide. It is proper here to state that these creeks partake more of the nature of running swamps than of common streams and take the place of regular streams.

February 27th and 28th, we did not move, but built works and made a bridge across Lynch Creek for the train to get over on, for the water rose and carried off part of the first one, built by the pioneers and the first troops that crossed. On the 1st of of March we moved 8 miles, and on the 2d we made only 4 miles to Black Creek, having to corduroy nearly all the roads as we proceeded. On the 3d we crossed Black Creek and marched 20 miles, still going northwardly. On the 4th we made 10 miles, passing the 17th corps in camp near the town called Cheraw, on the Great Pedee river and went into camp at the west side of the town. This was a nice town, or city, having both a river and railroad commerce, and here the rebels had conveyed a large amount of powder, ammunition and other stores, all of which fell into our hands, and of course it all shared the fate of the Columbia ammunition, the arsenal and most of the city.

We moved at 3 P. M. of the 5th, crossing the Great Pedee and went into camp at 9 P. M. The next day we remained in camp waiting for the rest of the troops to get across the river. March 7th we moved at 3 P. M. and after making 10 miles went into camp till morning. On the 8th we marched 15 miles, passing through Laurel Hill, and crossed the Wilmington and Charlotte railroad and camped that night within a mile of the North State Line. The country here is good. On the 9th we moved at an early hour, it rained all day and all the ensuing night. On the 10th we moved 17 miles, and in the afternoon we had a terrible hard rain, the teams all got swamped, and could get neither back nor forward, the wheels going down to the hubs, and we had to go back a mile, across a swamp to guard the train, and it continued to storm most dreadfully till about ten o'clock at night. The next morning we found the swamp overflown and had to put in logs and poles to be able to effect a crossing, so we only made four miles that day, and camped on the first dry spot we found at the late hour of 9 o'clock P. M.

On the 11th we marched 17 miles, crossing Rockfish Creek, and got into camp at 8 P. M., and the next day we arrived at Fayetteville, where we remained till the afternoon of the 14th, and sent off a mail, the first since we left Pacalliga, South Carolina. We sent this mail by return of a tug, whose crew had fought their way to Cape Fear river, to communicate with Gen. Sherman. At Fayetteville the rebels had also a large amount of ammunition as at Cheraw, and of course, it shared the same fate as that place.

On the afternoon of the 14th we crossed Cape Fear river, two miles below the town, and camped three miles from the river for the night. On the 15th we had another hard rain, but we made 10 miles and waded two more swamps. On the 16th we moved 12 miles, wading two more swamps again this day. On the 17th we moved 8 miles, and on the 18th we made 14 miles, and camped at 3 P. M. On the 19th we started at 12 M. and marched 10 miles, having halted for 30 minutes at 8 o'clock and got orders to march back. We turned back and marched all night and until noon next day, making a circuitous route, we joined the 14th corps, about 12 M. of the 20th, and in the evening we moved a mile, camped for the night, and drew rations, for we had been without anything to eat for more than 24 hours. This was tough, to go without sleep and without food, and march too, was indeed hard. We had marched near 30 miles.

On the 21st we moved to the front, and joined on the left of the 1st Division, 15th Corps, already engaged with the enemy. At 2 P. M. we advanced in line of battle and built works under the enemy's fire and within 300 yards of their main line, but our sharpshooters kept them pretty well down, so that the 83d only lost four men wounded. The fight lasted till about midnight, and the rebels then withdrew, and passed off through Bentonville, and saved themselves and us a hard battle the next day. This was a rainy afternoon, and in the morning fair weather came. On the 22d we moved 10 miles toward Goldsboro, and on the two following days we reached that city, by a route of 15 miles. We marched through the town and went into camp 2 miles north of it. This is a pleasant place, situated in a fine part of the "Old North State," on the Neuse river. There we had the pleasure to welcome back to the Regiment. our old Adjutant, Robert Love, for he had been of on a leave of absence since September. Sergeant George Dennison of company A, who was wounded at

Kenesaw, on the 27th of June, 1864, also came with him, they had both been on duty in General Schofield's army for several months, and came by way of Newburn, etc. They also brought about 60 drafted recruits for our Regiment with them; also Dr. Samuel M. Weaver, of Dillsboro', Ind., who was now assigned to the 83d as surgeon, ranking as 1st Lieutenant, and he has served us in that capacity with great acceptance to the close of our time.

On the 27th of March we went out with the rest of the brigade on a forage expedition, ten miles, and returned the same evening. On the 30th we received orders to report at Department Headquarters, in Goldsboro for guards, this we did the same evening. It is proper to state that we had drawn a full supply of clothing since we arrived at Goldsboro. This was what we stood in need of more than at any other time since we had been "in the service." We remained here on provost duty until the 10th of April, and took a very agreeable rest before starting off on another march.

On the morning of April 10th we joined our Division, and soon all was on the move toward Raleigh, to attack Gen. Joseph E. Johnson's forces. The same day we crossed the Weldon and Wilmington railroad at Pikeville, and camped a mile from the town, having marched 18 miles. On the 11th we marched 14 miles and camped near Lowell Mills, and before we left camp the next morning, we learned that General Lee had surrendered his entire army to Lieutenant-General Grant. This produced a tremendous sensation. A deafning roar of continued cheering rose over the camps, and thousands of hats could be seen going up fifty feet into the air, and others coming down at the same time. Some took the beef they had just drawn and hung it out on the tops of saplings they bent down and then let them up, and others strung some on bark, and two taking an end, climbed each a tree and tied it up in the air, twenty feet between the two trees, and left it there for the crows.

On the 12th we moved 12 or 14 miles, and about the same on the 13th, passing a deserted rebel camp, and leaving Smithfield 22 miles to our left. On the night of the 13th we camped at Broderick's plantations. On the 14th we crossed Neuse river at its nearest point to the city of Raleigh, (6 miles,) and passing through the capital " by company front," we went into camp four miles west of the city. This was the end of our pursuit after Johnson's army, for he had made terms of surrender to Gen. Sherman, who sent the terms to the city of Washington for approval. We remained in the same camp until the afternoon of the 18th, and then moved from camp one mile north of the city, to await further orders.

The city of Raleigh is a well shaded and pleasant place, and is surrounded by a healthy and fertile country. We spent our time pleasantly in our camp, going to the city almost at pleasure, until the 29th. On the 26th we were reviewed by Gen Hazen, and on the 27th the whole army was reviewed by Lieutenant-General Grant. About the

20th we heard of the assassination of the President, Abraham Lincoln. This produced the most intense indignation throughout the entire army. The deepest sorrow existed in all minds, and the greatest regret was instinctively expressed by all, both officers and men, except in one or two instances, but such men did not dare to give expression to any satisfaction, no, not a hint.

On the evening of April 29th, we got orders to march the next morning, for we had been notified by an order from General Sherman, that we would be conducted toward home in a few days, so at night the boys made a great demonstration of rejoicing, "for the war was over and we are going to our homes, from which we had been absent for nearly three years." Hundreds of canteens were loaded with powder and blown up, making a racket as of a hundred cannon. Rockets were thrown up, and many demonstrations of rejoicing were exhibited. On the 29th of April we "broke camp," and moved across the Neuse river. The day was excessively hot, and we were marched at a "quick route step," from 11 until 2 o'clock, and several men in the Division fell dead of sunstroke. This is no better than murder to the General or officer that did it, be whom ever he may.

We halted and went into camp at 3 P. M., having made 14 miles all this day. Thirty-minute guns were fired at Raleigh, in honor of President Lincoln.

On Monday morning, May 1st, we moved on toward Richmond, Va. The weather was fine and cool, the dust being laid by a gentle shower that fell during the night previous. We rested ten minutes in each hour, making our march pleasant through a nice country. At 7 A. M. we passed through a little town called Roseville, here we saw the "stars and stripes" exhibited from the dwellings of the citizens as we passed, this brought cheers from the soldiers. The ladies were collected from the neighborhoods to see Sherman's army pass, they showed every evidence of respect to us, as they wonderingly looked on the conquerers of the rebels. We made 30 miles, and camped near Louisburg for the night. May 2d, we crossed Tar river, and passed through Louisburg, a nice town on the north bank of the above named stream. We made 22 miles and camped near "Shady Grove Church." On the 3d we marched 28 miles, passing through the beautiful little city of Warrentown at 10 A M. The city was full of ladies to see the army pass. The "darkies" displayed a great deal of interest in the "Yankee soldiers," hurrahing all the time as we passed. One shouted, "Hurrah for de axletree of de whole world!" He seemed to think that the fate of the world turned on General Sherman's army, as the wheel turns on the axletree. Another shouted, "I'm glad de Lord helps you to do what you undertake!"

On the 4th of May, we crossed the Roanoke river at Robinson's Ferry, about 12 M., and at 1 P. M., we entered the State of Virginia. The river is about 1,000 feet wide where we crossed it on the pontoon bridge. We made 17 miles, and camped at dark by the Meherring river. On the 5th we moved 29 miles, passing Lawrenceville at 10 A. M. and arrived at the junction of two plank roads at 3 P. M., and also crossed the Nottaway river at that place, and camped 7 miles further on, and one and a half miles to the right of the road.

May 16th, we moved at sunrise, and passed Dinviddy Court House at 10 A. M., and halted at 2 P. M., 6 miles from Petersburg, and camped until the morning, then moved into the subburbs of the city, and remained in camp here until the 9th. On the forenoon of the 9th we passed through the city of Petersburg, and were reviewed by Generals Howard and Logan as we passed through. The city bore the usual marks of a seige; shell had pierced the houses in many places. We had crossed the Appomattox river by noon, and then we moved on toward Richmond. We camped at 5 P. M., having made 16 miles. May 10th, we moved at 10 A. M., having got in sight of Richmond, we camped by the heavy works that Gen. Lee had constructed to protect the city against the army of the United States until the morning of the 13th.

On the night of the 11th, we had a terrible storm of thunder and rain. The lightning killed six or eight men in the 1st Division of the 15th Corps. I should have noted the fact of our being marched in double column along the broad pike, on the morning of the 10th, so as to prevent Sheridan's cavalry from getting on the road ahead of us.

On the 13th we moved at 7 A. M., and passed through Richmond from 11 to a little after 12 A. M. A little girl continued to say as we were passing, "hurrah for General Sherman's boys, who were never whipped!" We moved on and camped for the night at Chickahomeny Creek.

On the 14th we moved 8 miles and camped at Hanover Court House. The next day we crossed the Little Pamunky, at the above-named Court House, and 2 miles further on we crossed the Big Pamunky on pontoons, and at 11 o'clock we crossed the Mattipony, and went into camp, 6 miles from Bowling Green, making 18 miles.

May 16, we moved at 6 A. M., and made 23 miles, coming in sight of the valley of the Rapahannock, of great extent and very beautiful, camping for the night 5 miles from the city of Fredericksburg. On May 17th we passed through the above-named city, and crossed the Rapahannock. We also crossed Acquie Creek and passed Stafford Court House, and went into camp after marching 24 miles in the excessive heat, many falling by it. May 18th, we moved at 6 A. M. and made 18 miles that day, it being very hot. We crossed Ocoquan Creek, and came in sight of the Potomac, marched through Dumphrey and camped off the road.

May 19th, we moved at 6 A. M., wading a creek, and marched 14 miles, passing two miles west of Mt. Vernon. May 20th we lay in camp all day. On the 21st we moved 4 miles to the west of the city of Alexandria, where we remained until the 23d, and then moved 6 miles to the "Long Bridge," preparatory to the great reviews of the 24th.

So, on the morning of May 24th we were ready to move at daylight, and at 9 A. M., began to "pass in review," before the highest authorities of these United States. Yea, and before the world, for there were foreigners there to see the "heroes of Sherman and Grant," who have been the means of saving this Great Republic from tumbling to ruins, and made this "form of Government a fixed fact" in the eyes of all the world. Our reception at the city of Washington, was indeed, a grand affair, and was worthy of the occasion. It was thought that 75,000 persons were there from abroad, to witness he review of the magnificent army of the United States. The ladies, especially, seemed to lavish honors on the men that had for so long a time, and through so many bloody struggles, through toils and dangers, taken their lives in their hands and had thus saved the fair heritages of the millions now living, and the countless generations not yet on the stage of action. They almost buried Gen. Sherman in flowers, and also threw flowers on every battle flag and stand of colors that passed in the moving column in the review, and many other demonstrations of joy were exhibited by the citizens on the occasion.

At 2 P. M. we were in camp, 4 miles north of the Capital; though we did not get our knapsacks till noon the next day. Here the 83d remained until the 5th of June, 1865, having a good opportunity to visit the public buildings in the city of Washington. The " Capital," the " Patent Office," the " Smithsonian Institute," " Every Man's House," were all visited by many thousands who never seen them until then, and there are many who may never see them again.

On the 1st and 2nd days of June, 1865, the 83d Indiana Volunteer Infantry was mustered out of the Army of the United States, and was furnished transportation home to their own beloved State, soon to be discharged and return to their quiet homes and to the embrace of their friends.

Company K, was not mustered out until June, on account of some orders.

CHAPTER VIII.

Before we close up the general summary of the 83d, we think it in place to append a few items in the line of moral reflections, &c., drawn from the nature of the subject we are treating on; and to this chapter, we think, belong some things as to the Chaplains of the Regiment, and also a more special description of the country through which we have traveled on our campaigns.

Rev. James M. Crawford, first Captain of Company H., was commissioned Chaplain of the Regiment on the 23d of October, 1862, and continued with us only a short time, for some time in February following, he resigned and returned home, leaving us to take care of our own spiritual interests. We were now without a Chaplain till on the 28th of May, 1863, when the Rev. Wm. B. Sanders arrived, at the rear of Vicksburg, and forthwith set about attending to the wants of the Regiment that came within the proper sphere of his duty, and indeed, he was very attentive in doing all he could for the comfort of the sick and wounded, as well as attending to the wants of those in health, and in the duties of the ministry, in preaching, &c. He formed a Regimental Church, and held a Sabbath School at Camp Sherman, Mississippi, in September, 1863, and continued with us till the latter part of August,

1864. He also re-organized the Regimental Church, and built a house to hold meetings in, at Larkinsville, February, 1864; but from some cause he became somewhat discouraged and resigned, and so left us in August, 1864, as above stated, and since that time we have had no Chaplain, but every man has done "that which was right in his own eyes." (?) So far as profanity is concerned, it is the "great bane" of the army, and thousands of noble young men of brave hearts, who never uttered an oath at home before a tender mother, or sister, or a conscientious father, seem, here in the army, to have lost all sense of that tender regard for the finer feelings of the soul that must preserve us all from this great evil. They will (many of them) surprise their friends when they get home in this respect.

And now, that the great object of our army is accomplished, the restoration of peace to "our one country" and our campaigning is at an end, a few reflections upon the result of the success of our arms, and the fruits yet to be gathered by, not only the future generation of our own beloved country, but by the whole world of mankind, may just here be in place. And first, a stronger union of feeling, and an undisturbed harmony of the States and Statesmen must ensue. Sectional interests and sectional institutions will no more disturb our harmony as a great nation, nor retard the progress of a better system of moral philosophy than that found in the standards of by-gone generations. This is one thing, we think, we have greatly needed, and we are in possession of lively hopes of seeing greater outbursts of moral and scientific light from the unfolding of the leaves of moral principle than has yet been seen by the races of mankind.

Our country has been struggling to free herself from the heavy guilt, and shedding much of her best blood, to wash out the stains which the folly and ambition of those covetous and power-loving men, that have infested our otherwise fairest and most prosperous country, from the first till the inauguration of this terrible upheaving of the passions of those wicked spirits, that have now lost both their power and their reputation; as the great masses have risen in the strength of their authority, and have thus dealt a death-blow to usurpers and tyrants. But we are now free from both, and all of these, and, as one great people, we now stand up before the Judgment Tribunal of the common sense of mankind, not fearing sentence for inconsistency or injustice from any quarter, whatever. May our sea now be ever propitious, and our sails ever spread, till the great principles of human liberty are cherished and enjoyed by every nation of the Globe, and the great blessings of peace and prosperity become continued companions in every social circle, and in every human domicil.

We congratulate ourselves in the thoughts that we have been campaigning for nearly three years, with the most successful army that ever marched against a foe. We have never failed of victory since the organization of the 15th Army Corps, except in the first instance—that of Chickasaw Bayou—and we have been in fifteen or twenty hard-fought battles, and in many skirmishes, and thus we have given our strength in sustaining the cause of human liberty and Republicanism, which are now fixed facts in the science of human Governments. Our Government is now no longer an "experiment," but must now become an acknowledged "fact" by all men.

Some may feel curious as to what will be done with and for the colored race, that have been an enslaved people here in our country up to the close of this war, the end of which has now come, and the "Southern Confederacy" has no longer an existence, even in imagination, but is "played out" and surrendered to the authority of Uncle Sam, "from the Potomac to the Rio Grande."

We need not feel anxious on this important point. They should, and will be educated, so as to be competent to take care and govern themselves. Meanwhile, they will be afforded means of accumulating a sufficient amount of wealth to take them to, and establish themselves in the Old World, from which they were brought, and thus they may become a "polished shaft" in the hand of Providence to enlighten "poor dark Africa." This is no more than just and equitable, and every lover of human justice can only pray, that some such things as these shall take place as soon as they can be brought about. It may be best for these ends, as well as for the best good of the country, to allow them some sufficient amount of territory in a climate most suited to their physical nature, for a length of time, sufficient for such purposes and ends. These we throw out as mere suggestions.

The patriotism that has been displayed by the supporters of the Administration, and by the soldiers and their friends at home, who have suffered on account of their absence, will compare favorably, it is believed, with that exhibited by our ancestors of the old American Revolutionary times. Nobly have our soldiers suffered, and valiantly have they fought, and they are happy in seeing such a glorious end of the war, and such beneficent results toward humanity come, as fruits of their toils and sufferings. These results, probably, no eye is so sagacious as to be able as yet to descry in the future, in all their extent and magnitude; but we think, we see in the Providential movements of the affairs of mankind, as directly connected with this struggle of our people, for the sustaining of "law and order," the "hammer" that is yet to "break in pieces," and the arm that is to throw down many superstructures of tyranny, and the fulcrum that is to overturn and cause to crumble down, many of the systems of proscription and sectarian fanaticism, that have so much beclouded the minds of men. Liberty is perfectly natural to mankind, and we take the ground, that whatever is perfectly natural is perfectly right, but liberty is not to be understood as to mean the right to encroach upon the rights of others, or of society, or the right to violate any "law of nature," or the "laws of order," by which the affairs of the Universe are naturally controlled. Therefore, liberty is that principle in natural law that extends to each person the immunities and benefits of all the natural world, without any right to abuse or to encroach on the rightful privileges of others; and the man that thinks that "liberty" gives him license to do wrong is only a "fool and a fanatic," and the man who supposes that it is his right to persist in vicious habits of any kind, is simply a badly-mistaken man, and is amenable, at least, to nature, and will, in every case, have a penalty commensurate to his crimes meted out to him. But I am reminded that I am not occupying the place of a lecturer, and I must desist from these remarks. We have all now seen that "eternal vigilance is the price of liberty," and, as American citizens, we should not, for a moment, forget the great lesson we have learned in this respect. We should ever be regarded as a people watching every attempted encroachment upon the liberal genius of our Government—the boon of the combined blood of our ancestors, and of our brothers and comrades in arms—ever watchful against that class of men and that stamp of character, that for so long a time disturbed our peace, and finally brought on us the trouble that is now subsiding so much, to the satisfaction of every patriotic heart.

As to the abuses of the natural rights of men, while in the army, I do not consider that the subject comes within the proper theme of this history, for we feel proud of being able to state to the public, that the 83d Indiana has always had such men for officers as considered their commands entitled to the best treatment as common countrymen and comrades, and, therefore they did not put upon them that unnecessary stringency that is so common among the officers of many regiments in the army. The officers of the 83d are gentlemen worthy of more than ordinary respect, and this I state without any man having suggested that I should make such a statement, and without reward. I say it because my own observation brings me to such a conclusion, and I hope that this sentiment is universal in all the Regiment.

It may now not be amiss to give a short sketch, describing parts of the country we have marched through during our three years' campaign, but nothing above a mere sketch can possibly be admitted. The south-eastern parts of Tennessee and the northern part of Alabama (for we were in no other,) may justly be considered the most fertile and healthy parts we have been in, though Northern Georgia is equally healthy. These parts abound with large springs of water, gushing out from the sides of the mountains and rocky hills, many of them sufficiently strong to run a mill, or afford water enough for an army. These parts are also very picturesque; the many high hills and lofty Mountains are adorned with huge masses of rocks, white lime and freestone, and in some cases granite, and pine, cedar, and other evergreens are thickly interwoven with the oak, hickory, &c., in rich variegation, forming a valuable variety of timber, as well as a beautiful scenery. Saltpeter caves and coal mines are also abundant in these parts. Northern Georgia is especially "sightly." Rocky

Face and the heights about Dalton, "Snake Creek Gap," in Horn's Mountains, ten miles west of Resecca, as well as "Lookout" and Kenesaw Mountains, are all worth the observer's attention. But Stone Mountain, fifteen miles north-east of Atlanta, is the greatest curiosity of all these parts. It is a mass of granite, bare of all vegetation; is 7 miles in diameter, round as a haystack, and rises to the height of about 3,000 feet, and standing disconnected from all other heights, it presents an interesting view as seen from Atlanta, Kenesaw Mountains. and from the Military Academy at Marietta, a once flourishing town three miles south of Kenesaw Mountains. It is said that Gen. Sherman taught in this Academy for a length of time before the breaking out of the war. This institution is situated half a mile south-west of town, on a commanding eminence, and must have been an agreeable place for study, as it is in a most healthy part of the country. From Macon to Savannah, Georgia is a remarkably level country, is very sandy, and interspersed with many swamps, and is more suited to the growth of cotton and sweet potatoes than to grain of any kind. One cannot but observe the want of fruit trees, which do not do well in those parts. The forests are extensive, and nearly entirely of "pitch pine." The plantations are small, and "few and far between." The swamps take the places of common streams, and have to be crossed by means of "fills and bridges." South Carolina is much of the same character as just described, "only more so." We saw but few fruit trees in the

State; but North Carolina is generally a good fruit-growing country, though the soil and forests seem much of the same kind as the two last-named States. Along the sea coast, the wide-spread branches of the live oaks, covered with the rich tapestry of Spanish moss, are an object of special interest to the observer's attention. Those parts of North Carolina lying around Goldsboro and Raleigh, and thence to the north line of the State, are slightly rolling, though hilly, and are quite fertile, and of that kind of soil the most easily cultivated; pine, oak and hickory are the most common kinds of timber that form the beautiful forests of those parts. From the Roanoke River to Petersburg, along our route, the timber is for the greater part oak, and in Virginia the soil seems to be especially adapted to the growth of tobacco, for on every farm, a dry-house (and often two or three) is to be seen among the most prominent appendages of the premises. But the soil of Virginia is proverbially a productive one. This is universally known, and therefore does not require a remark here; but, taken altogether, the Southern States will not compare with the Western States in point of fertility, or in the style in which they are cultivated by the occupants. But we look for a great change in this respect in the South. Thus we will dismiss this subject, and turn to notice the last days of the 83d in the United States service.

On the 1st and 2d days of June, 1865, the Regiment was mustered out of the service, but all the drafted recruits had been transfered to the 48th Indiana Veteran Volunteer Infantry. Most of these men were good soldiers, and men of good morals, though it was said that one of them did rejoice at the assassination of the President, but if so, he was the only man that did so in the entire Regiment. These men do not properly belong to a volunteer regiment, but being once connected with us and doing as good service as they did, they may be considered as entitled to a mention in this "little notice of our doings." We will therefore give the names of drafted men:

Company A.—A. J. Allen (died May 22d, 1865;) Wm H. Bendure, Henry Buckman, Conrad Bender, Thomas Barker, James Pepper, Francis M. Mathewson.

Company B.—James Cook, Joshua Cachley, James Churchill, Archibald Colwell, James H. Donaldson, Wm. D. Elston, Reuben Elkins, Hartman Eagleborger, William Fifer, Jacob Fifer, Albert Perry, Jacob Weber.

Company C.—Owen Gaskill, John Fabean, John Howard, Elijah Hummel, Joseph Ward.

Company E.—Herschel Ax, Abner Holloway, Wm. R. Jenkins, George W. Justice, Wm. Jay, James Jones, Nicholas Lemler, Alexander F. Light, Charles Ludwick, Owen Lynch, Wm. S. Miles, Curtis Overnan.

Company F.—Lewis Bowles, James Barton, Wm. F. Dunlap, Henry N. Hands, Samuel N. Hench, Azeriah Kilpatrick, Daniel Martz, William McGinnis, John McGrath, William Morical, Alexander Newhouse, Hugh Pickeral, Isaac R.

Personett, Henry Smith, John W. Smith, John M. Snider.

Company I.—George W. Bussard, George Pherson, Elias Rerick, Richard Scott, Richard Stone, James Stone.

Company K.—William Canaan, Graffis Abram, Isaac Hyatt, Peter Pixler, Henry Sutton, Spencer Spells, George Swafford, Daniel V. Shively, Aaron Stiver, John Stiver, Peter Vehler, Albert H. Taylor, John Gawkey, Adams Garin.

Thus, we have accounted for every man that has ever been a member of the 83d Indiana (unless we have failed to find the name of one man of Company B.) In the table of the companies, we do not give the names of such men as went into camp with the companies that did not pass the Surgeon's examination, and so were not members of the Regiment.

The entire distance the 83d Indiana Volunteers marched on foot, while in the field, is about 3,500 miles; that traveled by water is about 2,100 miles, and that traveled by railroad is about 1,100 miles, making a grand total of 6,700 miles. Some say we have traveled even more than this number of miles, especially on foot, placing the marching on foot at above 4,000 miles; but upon the most careful research I cannot find this last amount, but should be glad to find the data upon which to determine the exact distance. I cannot determine the exact number of days the 83d has been under fire, but it is at least two hundred days.

TABLE OF COMPANIES

Showing the names of the officers and men, with Promotions, Wounds, Deaths, Discharges, &c.

Company A. was raised in the neighborhoods of Milan, Pierceville, Delaware and Prattsburgh, in Ripley County. At its formation it mustered 101 men and officers; and musters out of the service 41 men and officers; thirty-six of whom were present on the 1st of June, 1865, when the company was mustered out.

Captain, Samuel P. Chipman. Wounded May 19, 1863. Discharged, April 26th, 1864.

1st Lieutenant, O. T. Darling. Died of disease, June 16th, 1864.

2d Lieutenant, Wm. H. Snodgrass. 1st Lieutenant, September 30th, 1863; Captain, April 27, 1864.

1st Sergeant, Robert Love, 1st Lieutenant and Adjutant of Regiment, October 30th, 1864.

2d Sergeant, Frank Dennison. 1st Sergeant, November 5th, 1863, 1st Lieutenant, April 27th, 1864.

3d Sergeant, Thomas F. Willson.

4th Sergeant, Henry T. Cayton, 1st Sergeant, April 27th, 1863. Died of bayonet wound, November 3d, 1863.

5th Sergeant, Clark C. Babcock. Discharged February 19th, 1863.

1st Corporal, Jacob Richardson. Detached Divison Q. M. Department.

2d Corporal, George Dennison. Sergeant, May, 1st, 1863, 1st Sergeant, July 14th, 1863; wounded, June 27th, 1864; 2d Lieutenant, May 1st, 1865.

3d Corporal, Albion Redlon. Discharged, April 3d, 1863; died at home.

4th Corporal, Wm. D. Anderson. Sergeant, November 5th, 1863; wounded, June 27th, 1864.

5th Corporal, Mack A. Richardson. Sergeant, Aug. 1st, 1863; transferred, V. R. C., May 1, 1864.

6th Corporal, Andrew McNair. Reduced at his own request.

7th Corporal, Jason K. Ransom. Discharged, June 15th, 1863.

8th Corporal, Frank H. Wylie. Sergeant Major, January 1st, 1864.

Fifer, Perry C. Engalls. Died at St. Louis, February 2d, 1863.

Drummer, Isaac Van Dyke.

Teamster, Robert S. Willis. Absent, sick since May, 1864.

Private, James Anthony. Died, Jan. 19, 1863.
2. " George H. Anthony. Wounded, May 19, 1863; discharged, Feb. 6, 1864.
3. " Alvah Blackmore. Transferred, V. R. C., Nov. 1, 1863.
4. " Theodore Brown. Corporal, July 1, 1864; Sergeant, March 1, 1865.
5. " August Bush. Detached Blacksmith, Division Train, March, 1863.
6. " John Baltman. Wounded, January 11, 1863; June 27, 1864; Corporal, March 1, 1865.

INDIANA VOLUNTEER INFANTRY. 103

7. Private, George Bean. Died March 17, (on boat, at Young's Point) 1863.
8. " Godfrey Brickey, Corp. July 1, 1863.
9. " Samuel Baldrie. Died at St. Louis, Mo., April 7, 1863.
10. " Cyrus Baldrie. Disch'd, March 6, 1863.
11. " George F. Beach.
12. " James H. Cleveland. Killed in battle, May 19, 1863.
13. " Edward A. Chapman. Wounded, June 27, at Kenesaw, 1864.
14. " James Coneley.
15. " Darias Dean. Died, March 7, 1863, at Millegan's Bend.
16. " John Drain. Detached Div. Pioneers, February 1, 1863.
17. " John D. Dashiel. Discharged, March 1, 1863.
18. " Samuel S. Day. Transferred V. R. C., August 1, 1863.
19. " James S. Davis. Died at St. Louis, July 1, 1863.
20. " James L. Fuller. Died at Young's Point, February 3, 1863.
21. " Thomas C. Fuller. Discharged, 1863.
22. " Edward Freman. Died at Young's Point, June 5, 1863.
23. " Charles L. Foster. Discharged, July 16, 1863.
24. " Joseph Grecian.
25. " Jacob Graw. Absent, sick, since May, 1864.

26. Private, William A. Hale. Detached Clerk, Gen. Hurlbut's Head Quarters, 1863.
27. " Zalman Hauley. Detached, June, 1863. Lieut. col. troops, November, 1863.
28. " Sidney A. Harding. Discharged, April 6, 1863.
29. " George Horton. Detached, Chief Q. M. Department, September, 1863.
30. " Alonzo Hael, killed in battle, January 11, 1863.
31. " William Hael. Wounded, January 11, 1863; discharged, April 27, 1863.
32. " Mark Hickox. Died, December 7th, at home, 1863.
33. " Samuel Hauser. Died at Milligan's Bend, July 4, 1863.
34. " Henry Hannegin. Detailed, Div. Train, October 6, 1863.
35. " William Hastings. Discharged, March 28, died at home, 1863.
36. " Samuel B. J. Syrigg. Leg fractured by wheel, November 6, 1863.
37. " John W. Jermans. Corp., Sept. 1, 1863.
38. " William Kelly. Transferred, V. R. C., September 1, 1863.
39. " John L. Knowlton. Discharged, April 17, 1863.
40. " Hiram Knowlton. Discharged, February 10, 1863.
41. " Leonard K. Knowlton, Detailed Division Pioneers, Quarter Master's Department, February 1, 1863.

42. Private, Peter Langvell.
43. " Daniel A. Langvell. Corporal, March 28, 1863; died, August 30, 1863.
44. " Thomas Leonard.
45. " James Merrill. Died at Memphis, Tenn., December 27, 1862.
46. " Daniel R. Marsh. Corp., March 1, 1865.
47. " Willam Mills. Transferred, V. R. C., September 1, 1863.
48. " Lewis Pennington. Wounded, July 28, 1864. Transferred, 1864.
49. " Joseph W. Parsons.
50. " Solomon G. Parsons. Died, June 15, 1863.
51. " Benjamin Percy. Absent since Feb., 1865.
52. " Oscar Richardson. Discharged Sept. 18, 1863.
53. " John L. Richardson. Wounded in hand, May 29, 1864.
54. " Jacob Risinger. Died at St. Louis, April 13, 1863.
55. " John Ranney. Corporal, February 28, 1863. Color Guard.
56. " Albert Rix. Transferred, V. R. C., September 1, 1863.
57. " John Roop. Transferred V. R. C., September 1, 1863.
58. " Howard Robinson. Disch'd, May, 1863.
59. " Adam Schornick. Died at home, September 13, 1863.
60. " John P. Snell. Discharged, Dec., 1862,
61. " Thomas J. Snodgrass. Detached, Quartermaster's Department, Feb. 22, 1864.

62. Private, Wm. Stegner. Disch'd, March 1, 1863.
63. " Washington Smith. Died at St. Louis, July 4, 1863.
64. " Hinkley Shockley. Wounded, May 27, 1864. Discharged, January 10, 1865.
65. " James A. Swift. Died, Sept. 25, 1863.
66. " Andrew Stoneking.
67. " Martin Stoneking. Absent, sick since January, 1865.
68. " James Thompson. Wounded, Jan. 11, 1863. Died of wound, Jan. 19, 1863.
69. " Robert Tucker. Died of Typhoid, March 1, 1863.
70. " John Tucker. Discharged, July 28, 1863.
71. " Jacob Tice.
72. " Conrad Ulrich.
73. " Albert Wayinger. Corporal, April 26, 1863. Wounded, May 22, 1863. Sergeant, March 1, 1865.
74. " Isaac Williams. Wounded, Jan. 11, 1863. Transferred, 1863.
75. " David S. Woods. Detailed Teamster, July 4, 1863.
76. " Louden Withrow. Discharged, 1862.
77. " John W. Whipple. Discharged, December 16, 1862.
78. " Adam Wynought. Absent, sick since October, 1863.
79. " Jacob Wynought. Detached, June 15, 1863, (Lieut. Col. Troop.)
80. " Thomas E. Wilson. Transferred, V. R. C., August 1, 1863.

81. Private, Leroy Wager. Transferred, V. R. C., 1863.
82. " Andrew Zwickel, Corporal, February 16, 1863; Sergeant, May 1, 1864.

COMPANY B.

Company B. was raised at and around Dillsboro, Dearborn Co. The age and patriotism of its first Captain, Jacob W. Eggleston, is worthy of note, for he was about 65 or 70 years old when he went into the service. It continued to be a strong company for a long time, but finally, through hardships, deaths in battle, &c., it was greatly dimuted; still, when it was mustered out on the 1st of June, 1865, its aggregate was 39 men and officers; present, 34 men and officers:

Captain, Jacob W. Eggleston. Major of 83d, March, 1863. Resigned 1864.

1st Lieutenant, Henry Girkin. Transferred to V. R. C. August 1st, 1863.

2d Lieutenant, Dandridge E. Kelsey. Captain, March 1st, 1864. Resigned May 2d, 1864.

1st Sergeant, Stephen K. Cofield. 1st Lieutenant, November 5th, 1863. Captain, September 5th, 1864.

2d Sergeant, James S. Shearer. Died, May 31st, 1863, at Young's Point, La.

3d Sergeant, Peter Rawland. Discharged, August 11th, 1863.

4th Sergeant, William J. Randall. 1st Lieutenant November 11th, 1864.

5th Sergeant, Stephen M. Bassett. Wounded at Resecca severely in arm. Discharged, January 13th, 1865.

1st Corporal, James Bruner. Died, July 10th, 1863, at St. Louis, Mo.

2d Corporal Henry Smitkin. Wounded, May 19th, 1863. Sergeant, 1863.

3d Corporal, Benjamin J. Wilson. Sergeant, 1863.

4th Corporal, John Opp.

5th Corp., J. Long. Discharged, April 3d, 1863

6th Corporal, James Bailey. Transferred to Marine Fleet.

7th Corporal, Ferdinand Sebring. Sergeant, 1864.

8th Corporal, William Lemon.

Musician, Darius W. Cooper. Discharged January 8th, 1863.

Musician, Lewis R. Hunt. Wounded, June 27th, 1864. Discharged, November 31st, 1864.

Wagoner, James Jewett. Died, August 6th, 1863, at Vicksburg.

1. Private, Ezekiel Abrams. Died, June 22d, 1863, at St. Louis, Mo.
2. " Isaac J. Alfry. Died, January 22d, 1863, on steamer Sioux City.
3. " Samuel K. Arford. Died, January 26th, 1863, on steamer Sioux City.
4. " James H. Abbott. Corporal, 1863.
5. " Washington M. Barnhart.
6. " William H. Barnhart.
7. " John Bennie. Transferred to 48th Indiana Volunteers.
8. " Thomas Butt. Died, January 20th, 1863, on steamer Sioux City.
9. " Benjamin Berry. Transferred to V. R. C. January 2d. 1855.

10. Private, John Cravens.
11. " Andrew A. Coleman. Detailed Div. Pioneers, March, 1864.
12. " Charles H. Clemens. Corporal, 1864.
13. " Edwin S. Cheesman.
14. " Jesse Daniels.
15. " John V. Dennice. Died, Sept 10th, 1863, at home.
16. " August Daman. Killed in battle, August, 31st, 1864.
17. " Zachariah Esther.
18. " Thomas C. Fisher. Died, January 2d, 1863, at Memphis, Tenn.
19. " Henry C. Foster.
20. " Richard Gray. Transferred to V. R. C. October 28th, 1864.
21. " Benjamin F. Gerrard. Discharged, June 11th, 1863.
22. " Joseph Gray. Discharged, February 9th, 1863.
23. " Wm. H. Gray. Wounded, May 22, 1863. Transferred to V. R. C.
24. " Jonathan R. Green. Died, May 1st, 1863, at Young's Point.
25. " William G. Green. Taken prisoner May 18th, 1863. Died, July 13th, 1863.
26. " David H. Helms. Promoted Sergeant for valor. Was in the storming party May 22d, 1863.
27. " James B. Hunt, Corporal. Wounded at Dallas, May 27, 1864.

28. Private, Joseph B. Hunt. Killed in battle, August 31st, 1864.
29. " John H. Hull. 1st Lieutenant of colored troops, July 15th, 1864.
30. " David Hess.
31. " John Hamilton. Discharged, February 10th, 1863.
32. " George B. Hess. Discharged, April 7th, 1863.
33. " Jacob Hoover. Detailed Div. Pioneers March, 1864.
34. " William Helms. Died, August 7th, 1863, on steamer Sioux City.
35. " Alexander Jones. Discharged, March 9th, 1864.
36. " Nathan P. Johnson. Transferred to V. R. C., May 15th, 1864.
37. " Ulysses Johnson. Died, January 8th, 1863, on steamer Sioux City.
38. " John J. Johnson. Killed in battle, June 27th, 1864.
39. " Daniel E. Knowles. Discharged, May 15th, 1863.
40. " Derrick C. Kerr. Died, February 8th, 1863, at St. Louis, Mo.
41. " John H. Leisure.
42. " John F. Linkmeier. Wounded slightly, April 21st, 1865, at Bentonville.
43. " John W. Leach. Transferred to V. R. C. November 1st, 1863.
44. " James Lindsey. Transferred to V. R. C. November 1st, 1863.

45. Private, William Meach. Killed in action, August 31st, 1864.
46. " James G. Mathers. Detailed Div. Pioneers, March, 1863.
47. " John McComas. Discharged, December 27th, 1862.
48. " David M. Minks. Died, June 18th, 1863, on hospital boat.
49. " Neal Maginley. Has participated in al the battles of the Regiment.
50. " Marian F. Mille. Discharged, August 1st, 1864.
51. " Wallace M. McClain.
52. " Henry Parker. Discharged, February 9th, 1863.
53. " Demas Perlee. Promoted to Corporal and Sergeant.
54. " John Pendergast. Discharged, January 29th, 1864.
55. " William Perlee.
56. " Amos Reymar. Died at Cairo, Ill.
57. " Frederick Roter. Died, January 18th, 1863, of wound received January 11th, 1863.
58. " Henry Roter. Detailed at Regimental Hospital, 1863.
59. " J. V. R. Rockfellow. Commissary Sergeant from organization of Regiment.
60. " Alfred Suits. Detached druggist, 1863.
61. " Joseph Sweazey.
62. " Geo. Spangler. Died, January 2d, 1863, at Memphis, Tenn.

63. Private, Reisen R. Sanks. Died, November 27th, 1863, at Memphis, Tenn.
64. " William H. Smith. Died, Februry 18th, 1864, at Memphis, Tenn.
65. " William B. Suits.
66. " Joel Sheppard.
67. " Sullivan Smith. Discharged, February 7th, 1864.
68. " John Spangler. Died, January 19th, 1863, on steamer Sioux City.
69. " John Shutts.
70. " Henry Smalksmire. Taken prisoner at Statesboro, Ga., November 8th, 1864.
71. " Thomas Sheppard. Wounded, May 22d, 1863. Transferred to V. R. C.
72. " John D. Smith.
73. " Isaac Trader. Discharged, July 15th, 1863.
74. " John W. Toph. Died, February 22d, 1863, at Vallard's farm, Young's Point.
75. " Hiram Thompson. Transferred to V. R. C. November 1st. 1863.
76. " William Wayt. Discharged, April 3d, 1863.
77. " John Thomson. Died, July 11th, 1864, of wounds received at Kenesaw, June 27th, 1864.

COMPANY C.

Company C. was raised at Rising Sun, Ohio County. It numbered 100 men and officers when it was mustered into the service, and at its mustering out on the 1st day of June, 1865, it had as an aggregate, 41 men and officers, 37 of whom were present. It had been peculiarly unfortunate. It had lost 31 by death in various ways. Captain Calvert of this company killed, May 19, 1863, and also Captain Benjamin North, now at home, deserves special memory.

Captain, Metellus Calvert. Killed in battle, May 17th, 1863.

1st Lieutenant, Benjamin North. Captain, November 5th, 1863. Resigned, September, 1864.

2d Lieutenant, Thomas Shehane. Resigned in 1863.

1st Sergeant, William H. Smith, 1st Lieutenant, November 5th, 1863. Captain, November 11th, 1864.

2d Sergeant, Ernest C. North. 1st Lieutenant, November 11th, 1864.

3d Sergeant, Edmund Miller. Discharged, January 7th, 1863.

4th Sergeant, Riley Brumley. Died, January 20th, 1863.

5th Sergeant, Eli Harrison. 1st Sergeant, November 11th, 1864. 2d Lieutenant, May 1st, 1865.

Corporal, John Bennett. Sergeant, February 8th, 1864. Died, July 24th, 1864.

2d Corporal, James Kay. Sergeant, April 15th, 1863. Killed, September 3d, 1864.

3d Corporal, William H. North. Discharged, June 18th, 1864.

4th Corporal, John J. Douglass. Sergeant, November 11th, 1864.

5th Corporal, John Monroe. Sergeant, November 11th, 1864.

6th Corporal, William P. Conner. Died, June 30th, 1863.

7th Corporal, John D. Sams.

8th Corporal, Pleasant M. Shafer. Sergeant, November 11th, 1864.

Fifer, Jacob Hess. Discharged, June 7th, 1863.
Drummer, David C. Thorn.
Teamster, Daniel K. Crandall.

1. Private, William G. Bailey. Corporal, November 11th, 1864.
2. " John W. Beaty. Died, April 15th, 1863, at St. Louis, Mo.
3. " John J. Brunner.
4. " Marion Brunner.
5. " John M. Callihan. Discharged, September 4th, 1863.
6. " Jacob Clark. Transferred to V. R. C., October 23d, 1863.
7. " William Cloud. Died, March 4th, 1863, at Young's Point.
8. " David Cloud.
9. " Henry Cloud.

10. Private, Theodore Scott. Died, January 8th, 1863, at Keokuk, Iowa.
11. " Oliver P. Cochran. Discharged, November 16th, 1863.
12. " John W. Conaway. Corporal, February 8th, 1864.
13. " Neal Conrad. Died, January 17th, 1863, at Memphis.
14. " Samuel H. Corry. Clerk for Quartermaster.
15. " Joshua R. Crouch. Division Pioneer, since February ——, 1863.
16. " Lanson Davis. Died, November 15th, 1863, at Memphis.
17. " Joseph Dodson. Wounded, May 30th, 1864. Died, June 6th, 1864.
18. " William Dodson.
19. " Edward Dodson. Discharged, September 7th, 1863.
20. " George K. Douglass.
21. " Arthur Douglass.
22. " Wm. B. Douglass. Discharged, August 1st, 1863.
23. " Samuel Drake. Died, March 17th, 1863, at Memphis.
24. " Jonathan Drake. Discharged, April 4, 1863
25. " Henry D. Englehart.
26. " John W. Facemire. Discharged, September 18th, 1863.
27. " Martin M. Fish.
28. " William H. Fisher. Corporal, November 11th, 1864.

29. Private, John W. Gregory. Died, July 29th, 1863, at Young's Point.
30. " Marion H. Hamilton. Died, January 3d, 1863, at Memphis, Tenn.
31. " Jacob Harman. Killed, May 19th, 1863, at Vicksburg.
32. " Hosier J. Harris. Discharged June 7th, 1863.
33. " Frederick Hess.
34. " Abner Hatfield. Discharged, January 31st, 1863.
35. " Joseph M. Hewitt. Died, August 15th, 1863.
36. " Henry Hewitt
37. " James Howge. Died, November 26th, 1864, at Memphis, Tenn.
38. " Michael Howge. Discharged March 7th, 1863.
39. " Richard Hutchison.
40. " Ernest James. Corporal, November 11th, 1864.
41. " John D. Roons.
42. " Robert Kyl'. Died, April 20th, 1863, on Hospital Boat.
43. " John C. Lare.
44. " Samuel J. Lewis.
45. " Peter Long. Transferred to V. R. C., September 1st, 1863.
46. " Edwin R. Mead. Died, September 11th, 1863, at home.
47. " James E. Miller. Died of wound, June 16th, 1863.

48. Private, Benjamin F. Miller. Wounded May 28th, 1864. Discharged Dec. 26th, 1864.
49. " Henry Monroe. Died November 26th, 1863, at Memphis, Tenn.
50. " George Moore.
51. " James Moreland.
52. " Jonathan Myers.
53. " Christopher C. Neal. Died February 8th, 1863, at St. Louis, Mo.
54. " George Nettle. Died September 2d, 1863, at Camp Sherman.
55. " James M. North. Corporal, November 11th, 1864.
56. " Henry W. Palmer. Died April 16th, 1863, on Hospital Boat.
57. " Oscar Parker. Discharged February 21st, 1863.
58. " Reuben Pocock. Died January 14th, 1863, near Arkansas Post.
59. " Franklin Roins. Died March 27th, 1863, at St. Louis, Mo.
60 " William H. Read.
61. " John A. Read.
62. " William Rex.
63. " John W. Rice. Died January 29th, 1863, at Jefferson Barracks, Mo.
64. " Cornelius Robinson. Died February 25th, 1863.
65. " John J. Rodgers.
66. " Benjamin F. Rollins.
67. " James W. Rush. Died August 25th, 1863, at Camp Sherman.

68. Private, Charles Sedan.
69. " Constantine B. Shaffer.
70. " Thomas J. Shafer. Died May 23d, 1863, at Milligens Bend.
71. " Joseph Shelly. Detailed with Battery, since May 19th, 1863.
72. " Silas Shelly.
73. " James O. Scipman.
74. " John Smith. Discharged February 21st, 1863.
75. " John A. Steel. Died August 22d, 1863, at Camp Sherman.
76. " Nelson Tarbox.
77. " Ernest H. Theas.
78. " William Waldon.
79. " John Ward. Discharged March 11th, 1863.
80. " John N. Weathers. Wounded at Dallas, May ——, 1864.
81. " Jeremiah Winters. Corporal, November 11th, 1864. Captured March —, 1865.

COMPANY E.

Company E. was raised in different parts of Dearborn and Ripley counties. It was also very unfortunate in sustaining great loss, its numbers were much diminished. It was also unfortunate in losing a good officer, Lieutenant Bridges, in its first fight. At its muster it numbered 92 men and officers, and at its muster-out on the 2d day of June, 1865, its aggregate was 38 men and officers, 27 of whom were present.

Captain, Robert W. Lloyd. Resigned April 17th, 1863.

1st Lieutenant, William R. Lennius. Died of disease, January 19th, 1863.

2d Lieutenant, Benjamin F. Bridges. Killed in battle, December 28th, 1863.

1st Sergeant, John W. Hamilton. 2d Lieutenant, January 1st, 1863. Captain, April 20th, 1863. Wounded, August 3d, 1864. Discharged.

2d Sergeant, Frances M. Gelvin. Reduced on account of sickness, February 9th, 1863.

3d Sergeant, Richard E. Blair. Died of disease, March 20th, 1863.

4th Sergeant, Benjamin F. Preble. Discharged September 13th, 1863.

5th Sergeant, William F. Gilliland. 1st Lieutenant, December 10th, 1863. Captain, April, 1865.

Corporal, Jesse Hamilton. Died March 25th, 1863, at Keokuk, Iowa.

2d Corporal, Jesse Cooper. Died February 17th, 1863, at Keokuk, Iowa.

3d Corporal, John M. Walker. Discharged September 25th, 1863.

4th Corporal, Marshall O'Neal. Transferred to V. R. C., May 15th, 1864.

5th Corporal, James B. Carter. Sergeant, September 9th, 1863.

6th Corporal, Darias H. Dodd. Sergeant, April 28th, 1863. Died October 2d, 1863.

7th Corporal, Henry Crouch. Died January 7th, 1863.

8th Corporal, Henry J. Craig. Died at Young's Point, March 2d, 1863.

1. Private, Oliver P. Andrews. Died January 27th, 1863, at Mound City, Illinois.
2. " Marcus P. Austin.
3. " James Burns.
4. " Herman Baley. Discharged, February 23d, 2863.
5. " Jayson A. Baker.
6. " Leonard B. Blair. Corporal, January 1st, 1864.
7. " William Boger.
8. " William Barton.
9. " Embly Burdan.
10. " Robinson Benham. Died February 16th, 1863.
11. " Henry C. Bostic.

12. Private, Huston Craig. Died March 2d, 1863, at Young's Point.
11. " William B. Curran. Died May 5th, 1863, at Memphis, Tenn.
14. " Joseph Crouch. Corporal, August 1st, 1863, Sergeant, November 1st, 1864.
15. " James S. Casey. Killed by a shell, at Arkansas Post, January 10th, 1863.
16. " Henry Ceigler. Discharged, March 2d, 1863.
17. " Jacob Dowers. Died January 28th, 1863, at Mound City, Ill.
18. " George Dowers. Died January 18th, 1863, on Mississippi River.
19. " Anthony Davin.
20. " John H. Davin. Died September 19th, 1863, at Camp Sherman.
21. " John Dust. Died July 18th, 1863 at Jefferson Barracks, Mo.
22. " Henry B. Davis.
23. " John Dean. Discharged March 16th, 1864.
24. " John P. Ebel.
25. " Mathew B. Evans. Died March 29th, 1863, at St. Louis, Mo.
26. " George R. Fisens. Discharged January 23d, 1863.
27. " Joseph France.
28. " James H. Gloyd. Discharged March 25th, 1863.
29. " Orin E. Gaunt.
30. " William J. Gelvin.

31. Private, Henry Grossman.
32. " Samuel C. Gilliland. Discharged August 3d, 1863.
33. " William Gray. Died January 26th, 1863.
34. " John Harper. Discharged March 25th, 1863.
35. " Lucas Hartrick. Corporal, April 28th, 1863.
36. " Frederick Hathaway. Died April 21st, 1863.
37. " John P. Ham. Discharged November 16th, 1863.
38. " James Hyatt.
39. " Samuel Higgs. Died January 23d, at St. Louis, Mo.
40. " John Hurt. Wounded by a shell December 28th, 1862. Discharged March 23d, 1863.
41. " Peter W. Hoover.
42. " James Harald. Died February 1st, 1863, at Jefferson Barracks, Mo.
43. " Barton W. Jamison. Corporal, May 1st, 1863, Sergeant March 1st, 1864.
44. " Nimrod Jollipp.
45. " John W. Kelley. Corporal, February 10th, 1863, died November 19th, 1863.
46. " Peter Lober.
47. " David Lotshaw. Died December 24th, 1862, on steamer Sioux City.
48. " John M. Long. Died May 14th, 1863.
49. " James M. Long. Discharged June 23d, 1864.

50. Private, Benjamin M. McKittrick.
51. " David McKittrick. Died March 20th, 1863, at Memphis, Tenn.
52. " Samuel Mink. Discharged September 12th, 1863.
53. " John Nodlow.
54. " Herman Neabe.
55. " Jonathan O'Neal.
56. " William Peterman. Wounded May 19th, 1863, died of wound June 25th, 1863.
57. " George W. Parsons. Wounded January 10th, 1863, died February 16th, 1863.
58. " John W. Roberts. Died November 21st, 1863, at Paducah, Ky.
59. " Elliott B. Roszel. Corporal, February 10th, 1863, died April 26th, 1863.
60. " Peter Renno.
61. " Tilford Rayburn. Wounded July 28th, died of wound August 24th, 1864.
62. " John Smith.
63. " Thomas J. Shreve. Corporal, February 10th, 1863, Sergeant Jan. 12th, 1864.
64. " Charles W. Spencer. Killed, December 28th, 1862, at Chickasaw Bayou.
65. " Daniel Scherer. Discharged March 12th, 1863.
66. " Joseph Sticker. Corporal November 1st, 1864.
67. " William B. Strichling. Corporal February 10th, 1863.
68. " Robert F. Thompson. Discharged May 23d, 1863.

69. Private, Lewis Whitaker. Sergeant August 1st, 1863.
70. " Joseph E. Webster
71. " Alvin Walker.
72. " Henry Whittenburg. Died July 26th, 1863, at Vicksburg, Miss.
73. " John Wolf. Died March 2d, 1863, at Keokuk, Iowa.
74. " Samuel A. Wolf. Discharged February 14th, 1863.
75. " Joshua S. Sterns. Discharged March 25th, 1863.
76. " William Lain.

COMPANY F.

Company F was raised principally at Versailles and Osgood, Ripley county, and in the neighborhoods adjoining. When the company was mustered in on the 4th day of September, 1862, it numbered 93 men and officers, 28 of whom were mustered out on the 1st day of June, 1865, twenty-one of them being present.

Captain, Benjamin H. Myers. Lieut. Colonel, March 1st, 1863. Killed, May 29th, 1864, at Dallas.

First Lieutenant, John H. Roerty. Captain, May 2d, 1863. Died, August 28th, 1863.

2d Lieutenant, Oliver P. McCullough. 1st. Lieutenant, May 2d, 1863. Discharged, June 28, 1863.

1st Sergeant, Charles W. White. 2d Lieutenant, May 2d, 1863. Captain, November 5th, 1863.

2d Sergeant, William L. Gray. Discharged, January, 1863.

3d Sergeant, George W. Ord. Discharged, February 28, 1862.

4th Sergeant, Nathan C. Harris. Discharged, 1863.

5th Sergeant, James Vincent. Died, April 9 1863.

1st Corporal, Richard S. Howlet. Sergeant, December 7, 1863. Prisoner, July 28th, 1863.

2d Corporal, Savannah Shoak. Midshipman U. S. Navy, January 15, 1864.

3d Corporal, Ezekiel Grecian. Discharged, November 21st, 1863.

4th Corporal, John W. Case. Killed at Vicksburg, May 19th, 1863.

5th Corporal, John M. Roberts. Wounded severely, May 19th, 1863.

6th Corporal, Amos K. Butterfield. Sergeant, February 10th, 1863. First Sergeant, May 2d, 1863. 2nd Lieutenant, May 1st, 1865.

7th Corporal, John W. Hobbs. Discharged, November 21st, 1863.

8th Corporal, Dewitt C. Faulkner. Died, April 18th, 1863.

Drummer, Watts H. Hunter.

Fifer, John H. Daubenhyer. Corporal, May 1st, 1863. Sergeant, July 30th, 1863.

Teamster, Tillford Folsom.

1. Private, John Anderson. Absent, sick since November, 1863.
2. " Samuel D. Ayer.
3. " Samuel Black. Died, July 2, 1863.
4. " Moses M. Banty. Corp., Dec. 27, 1864.
5. " John Beebe. Detached Wagon Master, April 2, 1863.
6. " Reuben Bevelhimer.
7. " Stephen W. Bruce.
8. " Henry Coon. Taken prisoner, July 28, 1864, at Atlanta.
9. " Jonathan Coon. Discharged, March 16, 1863.

10. Private, Adam Caplinger.
11. " Augustus Crulo. Corp., March 1, 1865.
12. " Geo. C. Cowen. Died, March 16, 1865.
13. " William H. Caplinger. Died of wounds, May 20, 1863.
14. " James Cregmill. Prisoner, Feb. 1, 1863..
15. " James W. Dickerson. Discharged, Sept. 7, 1863.
16. " John D. Dugon. Corp., March 1, 1863.
17. " S. B. Daubenhyel. Corporal, April 25, 1864. Sergeant, April 28, 1864.
18. " Samuel Bruner. Corp., Dec. 27, 1864.
19. " Edward Dermitt. Disch'd, Sept. 2. 1863.
20. " Henry C. Dawson. Died, May 20, 1863.
21. " J. H. Dickerson. Disch'd, Aug. 18, 1864.
22. " Wm. J. Fox. Died of wounds, May 26, 1863.
23. " Oliver C. Francis. Disch'd, June 20, 1863.
24. " Simon H. Fox.
25. " Amos Farwood.
26. " Ezekiel Gray. Died, January 2, 1863.
27. " Joseph Gray. Sergeant, December 14, Discharged, September 2, 1863.
28. " Joseph Gillman. Killed, Nov. 22, 1864.
29. " Ira C. Gillman. Marine Brigade.
30. " George Gray. Corp., July 31, 1863.
31. " Jesse Holt. Discharged, Feb. 6, 1863.
32. " John Hill.
33. " David Hess. Absent, sick.
34. " Wm. Huett.
35. " James Huett. Killed, May 30, 1864, at Dallas.

36. Private, John Hull. Died, February 22, 1863.
37. " George W. Johnson. Sergeant, Dec. 14, 1863. Capt. Col. Troop, Jan. 4, 1863.
38. " A. J. Kennan. Corporal, July 31, 1863. Absent, sick.
39. " Wm. Kenneson. Died, May 25, 1863..
40. " Charles Kennan. Discharged, April 2, 1863.
41. " Lyle S. Levi. Wounded, 1864
42. " John M. Long. Pioneer.
43. " John W. Lakin.
44. " John S. Luthey. Absent sick.
45. " Abram Ludwick. Died, April 7, 1863.
46. " Joseph Lingle. Disch'd, May 1, 1863.
47. " Adam Long. Corporal, July 31, 1863. Wounded. Discharged, February 19, 1865.
48. " James I. Mure.
49. " W. W. Miller.
50. " George Murry. Captured, July 28, at Atalanta, Ga., 1865.
51. " Jonathan F. Myers. Corp., Dec. 26, 1864.
52. " Thos. Moxley. Disch'd, March 28, 1863.
53. " Ebenezer More. Died, May 20, 1863.
54. " R. H. Neil. Discharged, April 2, 1863.
55. " Y. Y. Pullman. Absent sick, since June, 1864.
56. " Robert O. Neal. Disch'd, Aug. 29, 1863.
57. " Alex. Prible. Absent, sick, Returned, May, 1865.
58. " Samuel Reed. Disch'd. Jan. 25, 1863.
59. " Nathan Roberts. Died, March 31, 1863.

60. Private, Radolph Ray.
61. " John Radicon. Wounded, May 18. Died, June 9, 1863.
62. " William Rigan. Discharged, Jan. 22, 1863.
63. " Robert Rigan.
64. " Wm. Sadler. Disch'd, March 27, 1863.
65. " John Sadler. Discharged.
66. " Eph. M. Stevens. Corp., July 31, 1863. Sergeant, April 28, 1864.
67. " James Stillman. Died, April 20, 1864.
68. " George Strimple. Absent sick.
69. " Reuben Smalley. Corp., July 31, 1863.
70. " Peter Truitt. Corporal, May 1, 1863. Sergeant, July 31, 1863.
71. " Ephraim Wilson. Killed, Dec. 28, 1863.
72. " George Widener. Died, Dec. 16, 1863.
73. " John Watson. Killed, Dec. 21, 1863, accidentally.
74. " Thomas Willson. Died, Feb. 10, 1863.

COMPANY G.

Company G was raised at, and about Summonsville, Ripley County. It was made up partly of men that had been in the service one year previous and this will partly account for its continued strength. At the time it was mustered into the service it numbered 101 men and officers, and at its muster out on the 2d day of June, 1865, it numbered 55 men and officers in the aggregate, 45 of whom were present.

Captain, George W. Morris. Transferred to V. R. C., September 1st, 1863.

1st Lieutenant, George Oldt. Captain, January 12th, 1864.

2d Lieutenant, Levi Hazen. Wounded, May 28th, 1864. Died, June 21st, 1864.

1st Sergeant, Phillip F. Seelinger. 1st Lieutenant, September 5th, 1864. (For sometime Adjutant.)

2d Sergeant, Thomas M. Sunerville. 2d Lieutenant, May 1st, 1865.

3d Sergeant, John C. Kassen.

4th Sergeant, William Clark.

5th Sergeant, Robert Clark. Wounded, July 19th, 1863, at Vicksburg, Miss.

1st Corporal, Frederick New.

2d Corporal, Jacob Peters. Wounded, March 21st, 1865, at Bentonville, Georgia.

3d Corporal, John P. New.

4th Corporal, Habron Garrison.

5th Corporal, John P. Dunn. Died at Lawrenceburg, Indiana, November 4th, 1862.

6th Corporal, William Bower.

7th Corporal, Valentine Kehl. Wounded, June 25th, 1864. Died of wound, July 2d, 1864.

8th Corporal, Clark Wilks.

Fifer, Samuel C. Bartholomew.

Drummer, Andrew Hebel.

Wagoner, John W. Engle. Transferred to V. R. C. Corps.

1. Private, Christian Abegglen.
2. " Peter Applanap. Discharged.
3. " Gulliel Abegglen. Died May 16th, 1863, at St. Louis Mo.
4. " John Baumen.
5. " Jacob Bass.
6. " Frank P. Beresford. Died at Memphis, Tenn.
7. " Herman Barkis. Wounded, August 30th, 1864, at Jonesboro, Ga.
8. " Lewis Berger.
9. " Herman Bruce.
10. " John Bear.
11. " Nickolas Branagle. Wounded, July 28th, 1864. Died, July 26th, 1864.
12. " William Bush.
13. " Ira Klark. Killed, September 1st, 1864, at Jonesboro, Ga.
14. " Albert H. Clark.
15. " Henry Kaspens.

16. Private, Lewis Doll. Wounded, January 11th, 1863, at Arkansas Post.
17. " Lewis Dunn.
18. " John Decker.
19. " Theodore Dolle.
20. " Herman Dikas. Killed July 22d, 1863, at Vicksburg, Miss.
21. " John D. Erfman.
22. " John Englert.
23. " Anderson Fulcher. Discharged.
24. " Abraham Fink. Died of disease at Chattanooga.
25. " Steven Fellenworth. Wounded, June 27th, 1863.
26. " Erasmus D. Fulcher. Discharged.
27. " Frank Grossman. Discharged.
28. " John Gladvish. Discharged.
29. " Michael Gardeman. Wounded, January 11th, 1863. Discharged.
30. " Henry Gathman.
31. " Cornelius Hunt.
32. " Samuel Hummell. Discharged.
33. " Squire Hobbs.
34. " William Jolly. Died at Memphis, Tenn., August 31st, 1863.
35. " Alexander R. Johnson. Died at Young's Point, February 27th, 1863.
36. " Jacob Keil. Died at Memphis, Tenn., October 21st, 1863.
37. " Frederick Kras. Wounded, July 28th 1864, at Atlanta.
38. " Peter Krah.

39. Private, Thomas H. Kelly. Absent. Sick.
40. " Thomas Kinnan. Absent. Sick.
41. " William Lathrop. Killed, March 25th, 1863, at Black Bayou.
42. " Robert Lewis. Wounded, December 28th, 1862, at Chickesaw Bayou
43. " Abraham F. Manly.
44. " James D. Maynord. Died, March 25th, on Hospital Boat, at Nashville.
45. " Henry Meyer. Died, June, 1864, at Huntsville, Ala.
46. " Peter Miller. Died, September 5th, 1863, at St. Louis, Mo.
47. " William Mitchel,
48. " Frank Miller. Killed, May 28th, 1864, at Dallas, Ga.
49. " Perrine Moore. Died, January 26th, 1863, at Mound City, Ill.
50. " Jacob North.
51. " Valentine New.
52. " Alexander Oder. Discharged.
53. " William Oding. Wonded, June 3d, 1864. at New Hope. Died, July 1st, 1864.
54. " Peter Poppenhouse.
55. " Benjamin Plott. Died at Memphis.
56. " Ignatius Runner.
57. " Wm. W. Richards.
58. " John Rohler. Died, August 26th, 1863, of wounds.
59. " Simon Straly.
60. " Tilford D. Somerville.
61. " Frederick Schmidt

62. Private, Frederick Small. Died, December 1st, 1863, at Memphis, Tenn.
63. " Frank Staltz.
64. " Joseph Soll. Transferred to V. R. C.
65. " William Steinmetz. Transferred to V. R. C.
66. " Jacob F. Straly.
67. " George Schnetzer.
68. " Jacob Stealy. Discharged.
69. " Frederick Sparke.
70. " Reuben Stunmark.
71. " Frederick Trenelpole.
72. " Wm. Truckelman.
72. " Diedrick Thies,
74. " James Vaness. Discharged.
75. " Henry Weber. Wounded, January 11th, 1863, at Arkansas Post. Discharged.
76. " Jacob Waust. Died, September, 1864, at Rome, Ga.
77. " Philip Westerman. Died, October 3d, 1863, at Helana, Ark.
78. " Henry Wingerter. Died, June 4th, 1863, at Van Buren Hospital.
79. " Adam Whipple. Wounded, December 28th, 1862. Discharged.
80. " Phillip Seelinger.
81. " John Schmealtz. Taken prisoner in March, and returned, 1865.

COMPANY H.

Company H. was raised at Guilford and Lawrenceburg, Dearborn Co. As mustered into the service, it numbered 99 men and officers, and when it was mustered out, on the 1st day of June, 1865, its aggregate was 47 men and officers, 36 of whom were present. It has been one of the strongest companies of the Regiment from the first, all the time through. John Rawling is especially worthy of notice, as having been very useful in all works of a military character, and as having suffered the loss of his voice for more than a year past, though his health is good.

Captain, James M. Crawford. Chaplain, October 23d, 1862. Resigned in February or March, 1863.

1st Lieutenant, John Rawling. Captain, November 11th, 1864.

2d Lieutenant, Ferris J. Nowlin. Resigned, February 9th, 1863.

1st Sergeant, George H. Scott. Captain, October 23d, 1862. Lieutenant-Colonel,———. Colonel, April 1st, 1865.

2d Sergeant, Milton B. Wood. 1st Sergeant, October 23d, 1862. Wounded, January 11th. Discharged, May 5th, 1863.

3d Sergeant, Jeremiah Boatman. Died, May 22d, 1863, of wounds received May 19th, 1863.

4th Sergeant, Thomas Sykes. Wounded, December 27th, 1862. Discharged, August 5th, 1863.

5th Sergeant, John T. Douden. Absent sick, since November, 1862. Discharged, 1864.

1st Corporal, Daniel S. McCannon. Sergeant, Wounded, July 28th, 1864.

2d Corporal, Jonathan Novlin.

3d Corporal, John H. Jackson. Sergeant. Wounded, May 13th, 1864. Discharged, January 20th, 1865.

4th Corporal, Paul E. Hyatt. Discharged, October 10th, 1863.

5th Corporal, John Darling.

6th Corporal, George Herbert.

7th Corporal, Thomas Rawling. Discharged, February 24th, 1863.

8th Corporal, Alexander Baldridge. Died, March 8th, 1863, at Millegan's Bend.

Drummer, Christopher Philenus.

Fifer, George D. Horner.

Teamster, Huron Blasdel. Wounded, May 13th, and discharged, June 20th, 1863.

1. Private, Charles Blasdel.
2. " George F. Blinkman. Transferred to V. R. C., September 7th, 1863.
3. " William Broughton.
4. " William Boatman. Died, February 2d, 1863, at Memphis.
5. " Milton Bodine. Discharged, May 6th, 1863.
6. " Anthony L. Bledsoe.
7. " Thomas Blasdel. Corporal, September, 1863. Wounded, August 17th, 1864.

INDIANA VOLUNTEER INFANTRY. 141

8. Private, Thomas M. Craig. Discharged, December 27th, 1862.
9. " Robert Cassady. Died, October 16th, of wounds received May 20th, 1863.
10. " Robert Cook. Died, January 25th, 1863.
11. " John J. Colwell. Discharged, July 2d, 1863.
12. " Robert Cox. Died, January 28th, 1863.
13. " Wm. C. Campbell. Discharged, April 20th, 1863.
14. " Alexander Cassady. Died, September 27th, 1863.
15. " Joseph Cox. Disabled by a shell, December 28th, 1862.
16. " Christopher Ewbank. Died, April 18th, 1863, at Young's Point.
17. " Benjamin Elsing. Corporal. Killed, May 19th, 1863.
18. " George W. Ewbank.
19. " Louis Elter. Wounded, June 17th, 1864, at Kenesaw.
20. " James W. Freeman. Died, some time in 1863.
21. " Froz H. Frie.
22. " Caspar Feirstein.
23. " Jonathan Garrison. Transferred to V. R. C., 1863.
24. " David Giffin. Detailed in Regimental Hospital.
25. " John Griffith. Killed, May 19th, 1863, at Vicksburg.
26. " John Gahlert.

27. Private, Henry Hansley.
28. " William Horing. Left sick at Eastport, Ala., November 6th, 1863.
29. " Timothy A. Hiett. Discharged, April 6th, 1863.
30. " James Isgrigg. Discharged, February 28th, 1865.
31. " Philip Gahlert. Transferred to V. R. C., September 7th, 1863.
32. " Alfred J. Knapp. Corporal, February 14th, 1863. 1st Sergeant, July 31st, 1863. 1st Lieutenant, November 11th, 1864.
33. " Henry Kolf. Wounded, May 27th, 1864, at Dallas.
34. " James Kirkwood.
35. " Charles H. Kelso. Taken prisoner, July 28th, 1864.
36. " William C. Nopp. Died, February 12th, 1863, at Memphis.
37. " Seth Kelso. Discharged, February 17th, 1863.
38. " John G. Cahlerman. Corporal, July 31st, 1863. Sergeant, November 11th, 1864
39. " Jonathan Lewis. Discharged, January 3d, 1863.
40. " Enoch Lyness.
41. " James Lavy. Died, December 8th, 1863, at his home.
42. " James McDonald. Corporal, July 31st, 1863.
43. " James McCann.
44. " James McKee. Discharged, April 4th, 1863.

45. Private, William Maynard.
46. " Elias D. Moss. Corporal, July 31st, 1863.
47. " Hugh Maldoon.
48. " Henry Miller. Died, February 20th, 1863.
49. " Raphæl Miller. Died, September 6th, 1863, at Camp Sherman.
50. " Samuel McLure. Wounded, May 19th, 1863, causing amputation of left leg. Discharged, February 20th, 1864.
51. " Jesse McAnnon. Transferred to V. R. C., April 30th, 1864.
52. " John Probst.
53. " George H. Robinson. Corporal, July 31st, 1863. Wounded, May 27th, 1864.
54. " Richard Rawling. Wounded, June 27th, 1863. 1st Sergeant, Nov. 11th, 1864.
55. " John Rennert.
56. " Jacob Schelah. Accidentally drowned, May 22d, 1863, while doing guard duty on boat.
57. " Richard Slater.
58. " John C. Smith. Died, June 30th, 1863, at Milligen's Bend.
59. " Henry Sykes. Wounded, May 19th, 1863. Died, May 20th, 1863.
60. " George Smith.
61. " Jesse C. Smith. Discharged, August 29th, 1864.
62. " Mathias Smith. Died, August 21st, 1863, at Camp Sherman.
63. " James Starkey. Transferred to V. R. C., 1863.

64. Private, George Sibler.
65. " George Schile.
66. " Frederick Stephens. Absent sick, since May 1st, 1864.
67. " Andrew Shipe. Discharged, December 1st, 1863.
68. " Simeon Umble.
69. " Abraham Voltz. Died, December 5th, 1862, at Wiatt, Miss.
70. " Joseph Weibert. Died, on his way home, 1863.
71. " Harman Wehmire. Wounded, June 27th, 1864, at Kenesaw.
72. " Joseph Weekly. Discharged, February 18th, 1863.
73. " Platt Ward. Corporal, February 14th, 1863. Died, April 20th, 1863.
74. " Adam Zimmer. Wounded by axe cut in foot, on the works at Bentonville, March 21st, 1865.
75. " James Evans.
76. " George W. Fulcher. Wounded, May 22d, 1863, causing amputation of left arm. Discharged, August 4th, 1863.
77. " Frederick Opp. Transferred to 48th Indiana Volunteers, May 31st, 1865.
78. " Frederick Kuhns. Detached since February 13th, 1863.

COMPANY I.

Company I. was raised at Wilmington, Dearborn County. Some of the men of this Company had also been out in the one years service. When it was first mustered on the 4th of September, 1862, it numbered 91 men and officers, and when it was mustered out on the 1st day of June, 1865, its aggregate was 44 men and officers, 37 of whom were present.

Captain, Henry J. Bradford. Resigned, 1863.

1st Lieutenant, William N. Craw. Captain, March 1st, 1863. Lieut.-Col., May 1st, 1865.

2d Lieutenant, George W. Lowe. 1st Lieutenant, March 1st, 1863. Captain, May 1st, 1865.

1st Sergeant, George S. Johnson. 2d Lieutenant, March 1st, 1865. 1st Lieutenant, May 1st, 1865.

2d Sergeant, John H. Durbin. 1st Sergeant, March 1st, 1863. 2d Lieutenant, May 1st, 1865.

3d Sergeant, John B. Erwin.

4th Sergeant, James L. Smith. Died, July 18th, 1863, of wounds.

5th Sergeant, Joshua S. Christy.

1st Corporal, Charles Buffington. Sergeant, March 1st, 1863.

2d Corporal, Eratius Vincent. Discharged, January 3d, 1863.

3d Corporal, Andrew J. Huffman.

4th Corporal, H. P. Helphenstine. Regimental butcher.

5th Corporal, Howard Thomas. Transferred to V. R. C., February 15th, 1864.

6th Corporal, William H. Sloder. Absent, sick since January, 1863.

7th Corporal, James Duhn. Wounded, May 28th, 1864, at Dallas.

8th Corporal, Oliver C. Minich. Absent, sick since October, 1864.

Drum Major, John Baker. Transferred to V. R. C., February 4th, 1864.

Drummer, James N. Baker.

Fifer, Thomas J. Spicknell. Died, April 13th, 1863, at St. Louis, Mo.

Teamster, James F. Winkleman. Transferred to V. R. C., February 6th, 1864.

1. Private, David C. Beach. Hospital Steward, September, 1862.
2. " Benjamin Benham.
3. " James G. Adams. Wounded, June 27th, 1864.
4. " David Bordman. Corporal, April 21st, 1863. Prisoner, March 17th, 1865.
5. " Amos Bruce. Discharged, January 9th, 1863.
6. " Henry Barney. Wounded, January 11th, 1863, at Arkansas Post.
7. " David K. Bruce. Discharged, May 13th, 1863.

8. Private, Owen Canfield. Died at St. Louis, February 3d, 1863.
9. " Wesley Camfield. Corporal, January, 1864.
10. " William Chisman. Sergeant, January 17th, 1864.
11. " Clark Canfield. Absent, sick, since October 7th, 1863.
12. " George Calwell.
13. " John Clements. Wounded, May 19th, 1863, at Vicksburg.
14. " Jackson Chance. Hospital Ward Master.
15. " Charles H. Chrouly. Quarter Master Sergeant, from Regimental Organization.
16. " Oliver P. Christey. Transferred to V. R. C., May 31st, 1863.
17. " John E. Comfort. Discharged, October 18th, 1862.
18. " Benjamin Dressor.
19. " William H. Dean.
20. " James B. Flinn. Absent, sick, since December, 1862.
21 " James S. Fraser.
22. " Richard Falsum.
23. " John F. Goodposture. Died, July 15th, 1863.
24. " Jacob Goodposture.
25. " Thomas F. Toolpaster.
26. " Bavis G. Gay. Died March, 1st, 1863, at St. Louis, Mo.

27. Private, Charles D. Griffith. Orderly. Brigade Head-Quarters, since January 3d, 1863.
28. " Ebuero Goodrich. Absent, sick, since June 1st, 1863.
29. " Wm. A. Griffith. Discharged, December 27th, 1862.
30. " John Glass. Discharged, December 25th, 1862.
31. " Wm. H. Braston.
32. " Alfred Helphenstine.
33. " Phillip Hill. Wounded in arm and leg, May 17th, 1863.
34. " Verdosmon Hamilton. Died, April 5th, 1865.
35. " George House. Died, May 2d, 1863.
36. " John Howard. Wounded. (No date found.)
37. " Charles Holswell. Transferred to Marine Brigade.
38. " Marland B. Hazen. Absent. Sick.
39. " William F. Gillison. Corporal, April 21st, 1863.
40. " Robert B. Kirk. Corporal, April 21st, 1863.
41. " Clark Luizy. Died, March 18th, 1863.
42. " Charles Luizy. Died, March 18th, 1863.
43. " William Lane. Discharged, July 22d, 1863.
44. " Paul Lemuel. Discharged, February 28th, 1863.
45. " Thomas W. Morrison. Wounded, July, 1864. Discharged.

INDIANA VOLUNTEER INFANTRY. 149

46. Private, Williard Mendell. Corporal, January 20th, 1864.
47. " Jacob H. Oslage. Died, July 6th, 1863.
48. " Milton E. Roach.
49. " Thomas R. Rieler. Transferred to Invalid V. R. C., August 31st, 1863.
50. " Charles B. Sparks. Died, April 14th, 1863.
51. " William P. Sparkes. Absent. Sick.
52. " Pergil Shanks. Discharged, August 31st, 1863.
53. " Quincy F. Smith. Killed, May 19th, 1863, at Vicksburg.
54. " John W. Spickude. Died, March 7th, 1862.
55. " Theodore K. Stockdale. Deserted, November 8th, 1863.
56. " —— Smallwood. Died, May 12th, 1863.
57. " Henry Shuter.
58. " Daniel Smith.
59. " John M. Taylor.
60. " Ebenezer Vincent.
61. " Joel Willhall. Died, May 23d, 1863.
62. " George Ward.
63. " Christian Weisel.
64. " Lefole Stall. Killed in battle, January 11th, 1863.
65. " Alfred Maylor.
66. " Joshua Bell.
67. " James Welsh. Discharged, March 1st, 1863.
68. " George Munday. Discharged January 1st, 1863.
69. " Jasper Munday.

COMPANY K.

Company K was raised in Decatur, Ripley and Jennings Counties, and was not mustered till on the —— day of October. At its muster into the service, it numbered —— men and officers, and at its muster out, on the 3d of June, 1865, its aggregate was 39 men and officers, 28 of whom were present.

Captain, John M. Criswell. Killed in battle, May 19th, 1863.

1st Lieutenant, Ely F. Scott. Captain, 1863. Major, May 1st, 1865.

2d Lieutenant, James St. John. Resigned, April, 1864.

1st Sergeant, Wilber F. Hill. Sergeant-Major, November 25th, 1862. Commissioned to some other regiment in ——, 1864.

2d Sergeant, Nelson Johnson. 1st Sergeant, November, 1863. 1st Lieutenant, April 24th, 1864. Discharged.

3d Sergeant, Wm. R. Anness. Discharged, December ——, 1862.

4th Sergeant, Wm. H. Keeler. Killed, May 28th, 1864, at Dallas, Ga.

5th Sergeant, John Mixer. Died, October 16th, 1863, at Memphis, Tenn.

1st Corporal, 'Squire Brown. Sergeant, November 25th, 1862. 1st Lieutenant, May 1st, 1865.

2d Corporal, Recompense Carter. Died, May 25th, 1863, of wounds received May 19th, 1863.

3d Corporal, Thomas B. Mavity. Sergeant, September, 1864. Detailed Div. Pioneers.

4th Corporal, John W. Feighn. Sergeant, March 1st, 1864. 2d Sergeant, May 16th, 1864.

5th Corporal, John J. Rerfro. Died, March, 1863.

6th Corporal, John H. Kramer. Sergeant, March 1st, 1863.

7th Corporal, Jacob Ertle.

8th Corporal, George W. Abraham. Captured, May 28th, 1863.

Fifer, John Cooper. Transferred to V. R. C., September, 1863.

Drummer, Dennis R. Siglove. Discharged, May, 1863.

1. Private, Patrick Dugan.
2. " Philip Beger.
3. " Wm. J. Burk. Corporal, March 1st, 1865.
4. " Patrick H. Coleman. Discharged, January, 1863.
5. " Isaac W. Colwell. Wounded, November 25th, 1863. Discharged.
6. " John Calvin. Absent, sick.
7. " William P. Collins. Died, December, 1863.
8. " Theodore Davis. Discharged, October, 1863.
9. " Michael Doherty. Said to have joined cavalry, 1863.
10. " William Edens. Corporal, November, 1862. Sergeant, March, 1864.

11. Private, Frank Falkenback. Steward of Department Headquarters.
12. " Andrew N. D. P. Fuller. Accidentally wounded. Discharged, 1864.
13. " Aaron C. Fry. Died, April 8th, 1863, at Young's Point.
14. " Smith Furlow.
15. " Silas Gordon. Died, March 21st, 1863, at Young's Point.
16. " Archibald Goodrich.
17. " James A. Harald. Died, February 4th, 1863, at Young's Point.
18. " Peter Heigel. Corporal, September 1st, 1863. Wounded, August, 1864.
19. " James Hudson. Discharged, April 1st, 1863.
20. " Thomas Hudson.
21. " Oscar Hancock. Died, December 21st, 1862, at Memphis.
22. " Michael A. Jacob.
23. " James W. Johnson. Died, December, 1862, at Memphis, Tenn.
24. " John R. Jackson. Discharged, July 15th, 1863.
25. " Jacob A. Johnson. Taken prisoner, April 12th, 1865.
26. " Peter C. C. Jaques. Died of wounds, June 28th, 1863.
27. " Joseph Kopp. Corporal, March 1st, 1865.
28. " Rieley Garrison. Died, December, 1862, at Memphis.
29. " Nathan Martin.

30. Private, Frederick Myrose.
31. " Thomas H. Montgomery.
32. " David Montgomery. Wounded, May 19th, 1863, at Vicksburg.
33. " Jonathan M. Mason. Died, January 7th, 1863, at Memphis.
34. " Thomas McUre.
35. " Mervin McNew. Transferred to V. R. C., 1863.
36. " Philip Michael. Transferred to V. R. C., December 15th, 1863.
37. " John O. McNew. Discharged, June 25th, 1862.
38. " Alfred F. Myer. Absent, sick since 1864.
39. " Richard North.
40. " Henry Neve.
41. " Jacob H. Overturf. Sergeant, September 1st, 1863. Discharged, September, 1864.
42. " William Perry. Corporal, September, 1st, 1863. Color Guard.
43. " Franklin Rusk. Wounded, November 25th, 1863. Pioneer, 1864.
44. " Richard Rall. Wounded, May 28th, 1864, at Dallas, Ga.
45. " Lyman B. Randals. Died, December 24th, 1862, at Memphis, Tenn.
46. " Moses Rariden. Discharged, May, 1863
47. " Daniel K. Smith. Died, December 4th, 1862, at Memphis, Tenn,
48. " William Stech. Absent, sick at present.
49. " Andrew Stech. Discharged, December 25th, 1862.

50. Private, John Seifert.
51. " Philip Schwagler. Wounded, December 28th, 1862.
52. " Frank Slucer. Corporal, September, 1863.
53. " Charles Schultz. Died, March 30th, 1863, at Young's Point.
54. " John C. Thackrey. Wounded, March 21st, 1865.
55. " Jacob Vankirk. Transferred to V. R. C.
56. " Lewis Woodruff. Transferred to V. R. C.
57. " Jesse M. Woodruff. Discharged, January 31st, 1863.
58. " Frank Wagner.
59. " Conrad Wagner.
60. " George Willhelm. Discharged, February 27th, 1863.
61. " Anthony Weber. Transferred to V. R. C.
62. " Anthony Weber Died, April 18th, 1862, at Young's Point.
63. Frederick Waxman. Corporal, March 1st, 1865.
64. " Robert Wilson, Sr. Died, December, 1862.
65. " Robert Wilson, Jr. Died, March 21st, 1863.
66. " Cooper Gager. Discharged, December, 1862.
67. " Jesse Palmer. Transferred to V. R. C., 1863.

APPENDIX.

We must not omit to give here a sketch of our trip from "The Field" to our homes in Indiana; for though we had been formally discharged, on the 1st, 2d and 3d days of June, yet we were not disbanded, but were still "The Eighty-Third Indiana."

At 6 A. M. of the 5th of June, we left our last camp and marched into the City of Washington, and got on board the cars at 10 o'clock, and at 2 P. M. we were on the move toward Baltimore. Our train consisted of forty-six box cars without seats and was drawn by a single engine as far as to the Relay House, the junction of the two roads, that leading to Washington from Baltimore, and that leading from Parkersburg, Virginia, via. "Harper's Ferry" to the first named city, and known as the "Baltimore and Ohio Railroad." We arrived at this place at 5 P. M., and made a short halt at this junction, and the train was divided into two, so as to be able to ascend the heavy grade just before us and extending to the top of the hights between the above named stream and the Potomac River. At this junction the road makes the shortest curve, we venture, to be found in the United

States—turning at almost right angles to the left, and thence ascending along what we understood to be the Elk River; along this stream is a sort of town for several miles, and the scenery is grand, though artful and domestic, in the style which the citizens have clothed it in. This is a great manufacturing district; some dozen or fifteen large stone buildings, erected and used as mills and factories, are in close proximity on a canal created for that purpose, and the stream having a beautiful fall, it affords an excellent water power for machinery.

Ten minutes having elapsed, and our trains, containing the Eighty-Third and some other Indiana regiments and detachments, being all ready, we started onward, and by dark we had well-nigh left all the tributaries of the above named stream. Sometime in the night our "gravitation shifted," and by daylight of the 7th we had reached the Potomac River, and found that our train was standing still at the Baltimore and Erie Canal, and only three miles below Harper's Ferry. We soon moved onward, and munched our breakfast as we passed that noted place, not stopping to hold conversation about "Old John Brown" "or any other man." Harper's Ferry is a singularly appearing as well as a noted place in the history of the Rebellion. It is jammed and pinched between the sides and point of three mountain hights and huddled in a very small valley, it rests its elbows on the point and side of the mountain lying to the north. We were now ascending a heavy grade along the Potomac and continued to do so all day. At 8 P. M., we made a halt of an hour, for three or four trains to pass, and to subdivide our trains, still too heavy for a single engine to take up the heavy grade to the top of Cheat Mountain. At daylight of the 8th, we found ourselves at Altimont; (Mountain's Hight,) and an hour later our former train, or the same cars and their loads that started from Washington, were got together at " Cranberry Summit," and thence taken by a single engine along the descent to Parkersburg, which city we reached at one o'clock in the morning of the 9th, and laid down till daylight, taking a short and much needed sleep. At 8 A. M. we moved to the wharf, got on board of the Rose Hite, the nicest, cleanest steamer we had been on since we were in the service, and at 10 A. M. we were moving down the beautiful Ohio, looking with untold pleasure on the beautiful vine-clad hills of the " Old Buckeye State." We had now 320 miles to make by water to reach Lawrenceburg, the place where we were trained in "Hardee's Tactics," preparatory to our entering the arena of War. Our boat made good time, and at 5 P. M. of the 9th, we landed at the wharf of our destination, having stopped only twice since leaving Parkersburg; once at Cincinnati, only to "report" and send a dispatch to the telegraph office, and at Franklin Furnace Landing, 130 miles above Cincinnati, from 2 till 4 A. M., to allow the pilot a short respite of sleep, for he could no longer "see the Jackstaff," and so at daylight we were again under full headway down stream, enjoying the sweet morning air and rejoicing at the prospect of so soon mingling in the social circle of home friends, instead of "enjoying" the scenes of military life—the blair of bugles, the rattling of drums, and the startling long roll, the clash of arms, the roaring of cannon, the knapsacks, and the fatiguing march—all now past, we hope, forever with us—we have had enough of these things for one lifetime.

On all our rout, homeward, even from Raleigh, our way seemed to be attended with pleasant sights and pleasant things; the citizens, and especially the fair sex, all seemed to put forth their best efforts to give us a hearty welcome. And all the hills and fields were clothed in the rich bloom and green verdure of "spring time." The peach, the rose, the mountain laurel and every other sort of flowers were smiling and blushing at us as we passed rapidly onward. Sometimes a patriotic female would throw a bouquet of flowers into the cars, thereby showing the honors they would bestow upon the returning heroes of their beloved country. Many of the fair, in the blush of youth, paused not, but seizing the staff that held the banner of our country, they would continue to waive the stars and stripes in exultant triumph as we cheered them and passed on. The little girls and boys all seemed to have the same enthusiasm, displaying their little flags and cheering. The aged matron and the grand sire also joined in demonstrations of welcome to the returning boys who had now saved their long cherished country. Often mottoes were seen written in large letters on a board and nailed to the gate-post, "Welcome to our returning Heroes!" "Soldiers welcome to their homes!" In fact, it was almost an unbroken scene of demonstration of welcome to us until we arrived at Indianapolis, where we had a formal reception that will never be forgotten by any there present. The citizens of Lawrenceburg had no notice of our approach, until we were almost in sight of the place. Still they gave us a reception in the shape of something substantial, to satisfy the appetite; such as warm coffee, cooked bacon, bread, pies, cakes, &c.; a reception worthy of the time and the occasion. We were met at the wharf by our first Colonel, who was cheered before we had reached the wharf by a hundred yards. When he came in speaking distance, he said, in his own peculiar style, "What Regiment is that?" Three rousing cheers was the response. He accompanied us to Indianapolis, where we arrived at 10 A. M. of the 10th and took dinner at the Soldiers' Home, and were then escorted by the City Military Band to the Ordnance Depot, where we disposed of our guns and equipments, and were thence escorted to the State House, and came to a "front" of the Speaker's stand. Forty rounds were then fired as a salute to the heroes now returned, covered with victory and honors.

Governor Morton then addressed us, together with the 25th, 58th and 66th Regiments, and the 48th and 49th Regiments consolidated; also a Battery was present, and shared in the honors bestowed upon all the Indiana troops, by our noble

Governor, who has shown so much interest in the well-being and comfort of the Indiana soldiers, and in the glorious cause in which we have been engaged for the last three years. Our first Colonel also addressed us in a very touching style, reverting to the times of his command over the Regiment; our campaigning and sufferings; and wound up with some good advice and pertinent remarks as to the future. Major General Hovey also addressed us in a very interesting manner; then after a series of cheerings for the Governor and each speaker, in detail, and for the Regiments, &c., &c., we returned to Camp Carrington, to wait till Monday for our pay, and for our "Birds," all of which came to us in due time, and then we all went, "every man to his place."

The 83d left Lawrenceburg on the 7th of November, 1862, with 847 men and 36 officers; Company D was afterward added with 94 men and 3 officers. Total, 980 men and officers: and when mustered out at Washington City, on the 1st, 2d and 3d of June, 1865, the aggregate of men and officers was 372; present, 301; the balance of the aggregate being absent sick.

When we left for home on the 6th of June, there were present and started, 294 men and officers, the other five being sick.

The conduct of the men of the 83d on the way home and at Indianapolis was generally of the best kind for soldiers, and would compare favorably with that of others, yet there were a few who indulged in drinking too much, and of course some vulgarity and profanity was heard from a few, for a man that is rightly at himself can hardly indulge in either to any extent.

Pierceville, Ind., June 14th, 1865.

THE END.

www.ingramcontent.com/pod-product-compliance
Lightning Source LLC
Chambersburg PA
CBHW030256170426
43202CB00009B/767